Ribbon
Embroidery

A Craftworld Book

Craftworld Books Pty Ltd
50 Silverwater Rd
Silverwater NSW 2128
Australia

First published by Craftworld Books Pty Ltd 1998

Managing Editor: Sue Aiken
Editor: Laurine Croasdale
Designer: Vivien Valk Design
Illustrator: Annette Tamone

National Library of Australia Cataloguing-in-Publication data

Ribbon Embroidery

Includes index
ISBN 1 876490 01 2

1. Embroidery

746.44

Printed by Paramount Printing Co, Hong Kong

THE AUSTRALIAN
Country
CRAFT
SERIES
PRESENTS

Ribbon Embroidery

Craftworld Books

Contents

The Romance of Ribbon

Keepsakes to Treasure

From Times Past

Acknowledgments

JAN BOND
Lady with Bonnet

Jan Bond has an extensive collection of antique lace, clothing, purses, shoes and embroideries which she uses as inspiration for her work. Jan works part-time, studies Visual Arts (textiles) part-time at university and embroiders in every spare moment she can find.

JENNY BRADFORD
Rose Jewellery

After leaving England and a career in physical education, Jenny Bradford arrived in Australia and began a commercial needlework venture designing and smocking a range of children's wear. Doll and soft animal making followed, then an interest in patchwork and ribbon embroidery. Jenny has written numerous books on smocking, embroidery and teddy bears.

HELEN DAFTER
First Home Memories,
Spring Garden Ribbon Embroidery

Helen Dafter's love affair with craft began when she was young, spending her pocket money on fabric, laces and beads for her dolls' clothes. Trained as an art and craft teacher for primary children, she now works part-time teaching silk ribbon embroidery, patchwork and wool embroidery. For the last five years Helen has concentrated on developing new designs and techniques for garden landscapes using silk ribbon embroidery.

HELEN ERIKSSON
Bouquet of Roses,
Cottage Garden Embroidery,
The Essence of Spring,
Autumn Cushion, Field of Irises,
Lady Dreaming in the Garden

Helen Eriksson's love of embroidery developed into a career after her five children left home. Her skills in stitching and design are taught to students from her home in Adelaide, as well as other interstate venues. Her first book on ribbon embroidery has just been published.

KAYLENE EVANS
Roses for Ellen, Memories

Kaylene Evans has developed her passion for collecting old and new buttons, linen, laces and jewellery into a business called Kae's Treasures and Heirlooms, specialising in designing fine embroidery kits, many with hand-painted backgrounds. The bric-a-brac she collects are incorporated into romantic memorabilia pictures complemented by fine needlework and ribbon embroidery.

JUNE EVERETT
Wedding Ring Cushion,
A Romance of Roses

June Everett believes that there is no better finishing touch to a home than a piece of hand embroidery, particularly if it incorporates the added texture of ribbons. After a 19-year career as a teacher, June paints, and designs wearable art. She also teaches embroidery, and designs embroidery kits exclusively for Peppercorn Terrace.

KERON FATUR
Poppies in the Wild

When Keron's husband was involved in a serious accident, it served as the catalyst for her to consolidate her considerable sewing and design skills and launch her craft design business, Homegrown Works. She also has two books in the pipeline on gollywogs and silk ribbon embroidery.

BARBARA HALL
Nostalgic Picture Frame

Craft is a family affair for Barbara Hall – she and sister Carol make hand-cut and dyed fine silk ribbons for flower making and she recently attended an 'I love needlework' fair aboard the ship Queen Mary in Los Angeles with her other sister Judith. Barbara has a partnership in the Olde Barber Shoppe in Tanunda, South Australia, teaches workshops and has had several projects published in magazines. In 1996 she won Best New Product at the Sydney Stitches and Craft Show for the Vintage Rose Spindle featured in her project. She teaches workshops and has had several projects published.

CHRISTINE HARRIS
Bonnie the Bear Baby Blanket

It was during her 17 years living in the country that Christine Harris honed and developed the magnificent needlework skills she has today. As well as teaching embroidery, she demonstrates at shows, travels interstate to give classes and writes books on different aspects of embroidery.

MERRILYN HEAZLEWOOD
Tudor Garden,
Jonquils and Irises,
Apple Blossom

Although Merrilyn Heazlewood opened her first craft shop at the tender age of 23, she already had a wealth of experience in sewing, knitting and embroidery. She now teaches full time and has written nine books on both ribbon and wool embroidery.

HEATHER JOYNES
Basket of Flowers

Heather Joynes has tutored throughout the world on embroidery and her work has been shown in art galleries and exhibitions in Australia. An avid antique needlework tool collector, teacher and author, Heather has completed her seventh book _Favourite Flowers,_ published by Kangaroo Press.

ANNIE LONDON & SUSAN KAROLY
Edwardian Cottage

Annie London, a graphic artist, and Susan Karoly, a quiltmaker, have combined their skills to promote the modern form of trapunto – a stitching technique used in this project. They work as a team producing and promoting shadow trapunto designs and kits and now supply more than 250 specialist craft shops.

LYNDA MAKER
Victorian Scissors Case and Pincushion

Using the skills developed during a previous career in graphic design, Lynda Maker now designs her own embroidery pieces, teaches, demonstrates at craft shows and writes for magazines. She is always on the lookout for something old or unusual and loves creating pieces that evoke the antiquated beauty of the 1900s.

GLORIA MCKINNON
Lace and Roses Needlework Set,
Peony Rose Pillow

After 20 years in the world of needlework and crafts, Gloria McKinnon's energy and enthusiasm are undimmed. Anne's Glory Box, her Newcastle store, is a mecca for stitchers, quilters and craftspeople alike. Gloria seems to be in perpetual motion with lightning trips around Australia and overseas to attend craft shows, and teaching classes and workshops.

ELIZABETH MOIR
Bouquet of Pastel Favourites

Elizabeth Moir has made craft her life and ribbon embroidery is a specialty. As well as producing beautiful work she teaches ribbon embroidery both nationally and internationally, as well as running a mail order business, French Ribbons and Roses, and takes groups to France annually to visit silk museums, tapestry workshops and ribbon shops.

SUE STROM
Floral Fantasy

Sue Strom cannot remember a time when she was not sewing. Over the years Sue has refined her talents and techniques and now concentrates on teaching heirloom sewing, smocking and embroidery. She also writes for craft and needlework magazines and has published her own collection of embroidery designs.

KIRRY TOOSE
A Victorian Reticule

Kirry Toose has been teaching embroidery, craft, wearable art and découpage for the last eight years in Sydney. Formally trained in dress design and pattern making, Kirry is a self-confessed bower bird who constantly searches out collectables from second-hand and antique shops as inspiration for her romantic cushions, decorated boxes and exquisite embroidery.

JOAN WATTERS
Cherub Cushion

Joan Watters trained as a dressmaker and ran her own dressmaking business from home. This interest developed into embroidery and she is now a full-time teacher, designer and author. Joan designs and markets kits for emboidered bears, blankets and cushions through her business Delwood Designs.

Introduction

A quiet evening in front of the fire, a lazy afternoon on holiday or simply a communal morning amongst friends is how many of us come to enjoy, share and learn a craft. Ribbon embroidery is no different. Revived in the last decade, this superb craft has been enthusiastically welcomed and now holds its rightful place in the homes and hearts of embroiderers keen to develop their skill and display their finished works.

Ribbon embroidery is relatively inexpensive and can be done anywhere. Once the basics have been learnt, there is wide scope for different designs, especially when combined with thread embroidery.

Throughout the book there are beautiful colour photographs, clear concise instructions, stitch diagrams and pattern illustrations with information on how to enlarge each piece so it can be used at actual size. A pull-out pattern sheet has been provided for the larger patterns.

Ribbon Embroidery will appeal to embroiderers with all levels of experience. It combines a stunning selection of designs using the most simple stitches for absolute beginners with the more challenging and complex projects for very experienced stitchers. The one common thread is that *Ribbon Embroidery* offers many inspiring ideas that will stimulate and encourage you to develop your own design skills and play with colour combinations.

Beginners will find the reference section at the rear of the book extremely helpful in getting started. By following the Basic Essentials information of equipment with suggestions for using certain threads and fabrics, beginners will be able to equip themselves easily and learn how to maintain their work tools.

The Stitch Guide is another handy reference tool. It has clear, illustrated diagrams of all the stitches required for ribbon embroidery, while specific techniques are presented with projects. An experienced embroiderer may find this a helpful check list but for the beginner it is invaluable. Before spending your money buying materials for a specific project, use the Stitch Guide to check which stitches you will be using and then practise the stitches until you are competent and your tension is correct. The more time spent at this vital stage will pay dividends when you start working on your fabric.

In *Ribbon Embroidery* we showcase Australia's most talented and diverse embroiderers. Many of the contributors also teach embroidery, make retail kits for enthusiasts, and write books about embroidery in general and ribbon embroidery in particular. A brief profile of each contributor can be found at the beginning of the book.

The book is divided into three themes: The Romance of Ribbon, when all that is whimsical and romantic is depicted in the beauty of ribbon; Keepsakes to Treasure – using ribbon and complementary embroidery to create pieces that can be handed down through generations of the family; and From Times Past – showing how ribbon embroidery can create a timeless piece that evokes the nostalgia of the past – be it your memories or images you hold dear.

Ribbon Embroidery is the perfect book for anyone who appreciates or enjoys working with ribbon.

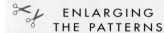

ENLARGING THE PATTERNS

Most patterns in this book need to be enlarged before use. To do this accurately, look for the photocopy symbol and number on the pattern (for example ▱ 130%), set the photocopier to the percentage given and photocopy each piece on this setting. Patterns that have the symbol ▱ SS (Same Size) do not need enlarging.

Silk Ribbons
throughout History

Around 1200 BC the Chinese stumbled across the secret of producing silk. It was a much sought-after commodity and they jealously guarded the secret of its production. The Chinese established a trade monopoly throughout the world by sending caravans laden with raw fibres and finished fabrics across the Huang River and along the treacherous Old Silk Road to the shores of the Mediterranean. The conditions were harsh and dangerous and the journey could take two years or more. Consequently, silk was a great luxury – its price was on a par with gold – and the secrets of its manufacture were hidden from envious nations for centuries.

The Romans thought that silk grew on trees and Pliny noted that "the Seres are famous for the wool of their forests. They remove the down from leaves with the help of water."

Finally, during the reign of Emperor Justinian, two Indian monks hid silkworm cocoons and mulberry tree shoots in hollow bamboo tubes and smuggled them out of China. A silk industry was quickly established in Byzantium, opening up a world-wide industry and smashing the Chinese monopoly.

From this point, France, Germany, Italy and Britain began weaving ribbon for dress trimmings and sashes and at the end of the 16th century an Englishman invented a loom which could weave 20 ribbons simultaneously. Some ribbons were woven with gold or silver thread and at different periods in history it was considered illegal for anyone but nobility to be seen wearing ribbons.

By the mid-17th century, ribbons were especially popular with men and became the accepted status symbol of the idle rich in France and England. In Colonial America, very little ribbon was worn by those who held anti-English sentiments and it wasn't until 1815 that the

first ribbon factory opened for business in the New World.

Towards the end of the 18th century ribbon embroidery was used on the elaborate costumes in the European courts. Portraits of Queen Marie Antoinette of France and Madame de Pompadour, who was considered a leader of fashion, depict gowns trimmed with rows of bows and floral swags, together with handmade lace ruffles and edgings.

Ribbon work was prominently featured throughout Victorian times when it became a more domestic craft and ribbon embellishment found its way onto all manner of household items and small accessories and mementos. Ribbon was used lavishly to decorate Victorian costumes although it was in the field of millinery that this craft really came into its own.

Revived in popularity around the end of the 19th century, ribbons were a popular decoration in crazy patchwork. Ribbon work on a black velvet or satin background also became popular around this time. Made up into framed pictures or women's bags, there are still some beautiful examples of this work to be seen today, though the intensity of some of the ribbon colours may have faded.

For most of the 20th century, ribbon embroidery has been neglected. The widely available satin and nylon ribbons lack the flexibility and soft qualities of silk and it was not until about 10 years ago that the craft was revived in Australia. The craft has since flourished as it is quick and easy to learn, offers a wide scope of uses and gives a sense of achievement to experienced ribbon embroiderers and beginners alike.

The Romance of Ribbon

Over the centuries ribbons have been woven into our lives as tokens of love, ceremonial symbols associated with prizes and medals, garment embellishments or associated with romantic celebrations such as the ancient art of Maypole dancing.

Wedding Ring Cushion

*Designed in rich shades of cream, highlighted by organdy,
rayon and silk ribbon, pearls and seed beads, this Wedding Ring Cushion
is a charming idea that's both practical on the day
and a keepsake to treasure forever.*

PREPARATION

From dupion silk, cut cushion heart shapes and two frill strips 21cm (8in) x width of fabric. See cutting layout below.

Cut out the heart embroidery template on page 18. Use it as a guide to tack a heart shape at the centre of the fabric with ordinary cream sewing thread.

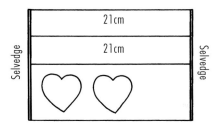

Cutting layout

EMBROIDERY

Attach 8mm (³⁄₈in) tea-dyed cream rayon ribbon in lattice design following the placement guide on page 20. Stitch to the edges of the embroidery template outline and catch each cross-over point with a small, secure stitch.

RIBBON ROSES, BUDS AND LEAVES

Following the instructions and diagrams on page 16, make all the ribbon roses and ribbon leaves. Attach the roses according to the placement guide, beginning with the largest of the roses and working to the smallest. Attach the leaves, ensuring the raw edges are hidden under the roses and well secured.

SPIDER'S WEB FLOWER SPRAYS

Make Spider's Web flowers in 4mm (⅛in) cream silk ribbon. Refer to Stitch Guide page 160. Using ordinary sewing

thread, work five spokes as shown. Bring No 8 crewel needle and ribbon to front of work, as close as possible to the centre of the spokes. Begin weaving the ribbon under and over the spokes (taking ribbon between the spokes and surface of the fabric), working from the centre out and keeping the stitches loose. The spokes for the largest flower of the spray should be 5mm (¼in) long, reducing slightly for the next flower. With the same ribbon, work three Straight Stitches for the buds.

The leaves are Satin Stitched using two or, if you prefer extra texture, three threads of olive green cotton and No 8 crewel needle. Refer to Stitch Guide page 160. Begin stitching on the left side of the leaf, stitching up towards the tip.

Keep the stitches fairly loose to give texture to your work and to prevent puckering the backing fabric. The stitches are on a steeper angle as you move up the leaf. Complete the stitches on one side, then stitch down the other side to complete the leaf. Using two strands of olive green embroidery cotton, work Straight Stitch stems.

BULLION SPRAYS

Work the Bullions using three strands of cream embroidery cotton and No 8 crewel needle. The largest flower has three Bullions of eight or nine wraps. The second flower has three Bullions of five or six wraps. Finish the spray with a French Knot. The leaves and stems are Straight Stitched in two strands of olive green cotton. For the leaves, work three or five stitches, with the centre stitch longer than the side stitches.

Attach pearl and seed bead clusters, using a single cream sewing thread and No 10 crewel needle. Attach a small pearl where each of the lattice ribbons crosses over, hiding the stitch that secures the ribbons.

Cut two 35cm x 4mm (14in x ⅛in) lengths of cream silk ribbon, for ring bows. Using placement guide, attach with

FINISHED SIZE

- 28cm x 49cm (11in x 19in)

MATERIALS

- 70cm (³⁄₄yd) cream dupion silk
- 30cm (³⁄₈yd) cream or white poly poplin fabric for insert
- 25cm x 35mm (¹⁄₄yd x 1½in) Pan Pacific cream organdy ribbon with gold edge (See Note)
- 2.4m x 25mm (2⁵⁄₈yd x 1in) Pan Pacific cream satin-edged organdy ribbon
- 70cm x 25mm (³⁄₄yd x 1in) Pan Pacific olive organdy ribbon
- 1.6m x 13mm (1³⁄₄yd x ½in) Mokuba cream rayon ribbon (tea-dyed — see Helpful Hint)
- 40cm x 13mm (½yd x ½in) Mokuba pale gold rayon ribbon
- 1.8m x 8mm (2yd x ³⁄₈in) Mokuba cream rayon ribbon (tea-dyed)
- 60cm x 7mm (⁵⁄₈yd x ¼in) YLI cream silk ribbon
- 40cm x 15mm (½yd x ⁵⁄₈in) Mokuba sheer gold-edged ribbon
- 1.8m x 4mm (2yd x ⅛in) YLI cream silk ribbon
- DMC Stranded Embroidery Cotton: one skein each of cream (3774), dark golden olive (830)
- Cream pearls: approximately 35 large, 90 small
- Mill Hill antique seed beads: one packet gold (03039)
- Polyester filling
- Cream sewing thread
- No 8 and 10 crewel needles

NOTE: the gold-edged organdy ribbon is for the back of the cushion and is only required if you are using your cushion as a ring cushion.

STITCHES USED

Folded Ribbon Rose, Spider's Web Rose, Straight Stitch, Satin Stitch, Bullion Stitch, French Knot

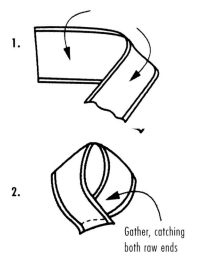

1.

2.

Gather, catching
both raw ends

Cut 4cm (1½in) lengths of ribbon. Fold
each end forward and slightly down towards
the centre. Gather raw edges with running
stitch. Stitch securely to backing fabric
under the edge of a rose, ensuring all raw
edges are hidden.

Ribbon leaves

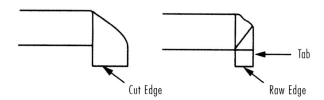

Cut Edge   Raw Edge   Tab

1. Fold ribbon diagonally so a short tab of ribbon
comes below the bottom edge.

2. Fold the folded section in half again.

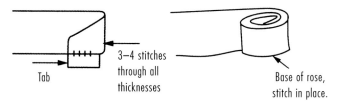

3–4 stitches
through all
thicknesses

Tab

Base of rose,
stitch in place.

3. Fold entire folded section over again. Stitch
in place at base using single sewing thread.

4. Make three more folds, each a little larger
than the previous one. Stitch ribbon in place
at base of rose through all thicknesses.
Stitch sides of base in, to keep a rounded
shape.

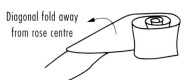

Diagonal fold away
from rose centre

5. Hold rose centre in right hand. Use left hand to
fold ribbon in a long diagonal fold away from
rose centre. Use right hand to turn rose centre
so that diagonal fold wraps about halfway
around the rose. Stitch the edge of new ribbon
fold to side of rose base.

6. Continue diagonal folding and wrapping until
3–4 wraps have been completed and stitched.
After final fold, cut ribbon leaving a short tab.
Tuck this end under rose and stitch in place.
Leave thread attached to stitch rose to work.
Use slip stitches all around the base of the
rose, tucking in any raw edges as you stitch.
Secure with 3 or 4 stitches on wrong side.

Folded Ribbon Rose

small but secure stitches, slightly off-
centre of the length of ribbon so that the
tails will be different lengths.

MAKING UP

Stitch the 21cm (8in) frill strips together
with flat, open seams, forming a complete circle. Stitch 35mm (1½in) sheer,
gold-edged ribbon to back of cushion, a
little more than halfway up. Attach ribbon
at sides only – this is for holding the ring
cushion. If this cushion is not intended as
a ring cushion, omit this step.

Fold the frill by placing the wrong
sides together.

Stitch two rows of machine gathering
close to the raw edges of the frill. The
gathering will be easier if the stitching is
in two or three sections. Gather frill to fit
around the edge of the cushion.

Pin frill to front edge of cushion, with
raw edges together. Stitch frill to cushion.

Place and pin the cushion back over
the front section, with the right sides

together. Stitch, ensuring you leave a gap of approximately 8–10cm (3¼in–4in) on one side close to base of cushion for turning. Turn cushion to right side. Make an insert the same size as the cushion. Fill firmly with polyester filling and stitch closed. Place insert inside cushion and, using cream sewing thread and fine slip stitches, hand-stitch cushion to close gap.

 HELPFUL HINT

A simple way to hand-dye Mokuba rayon ribbon is by using tea. Dip a tea bag into half a cup of boiling water until it is very strong. Soak the ribbons for three minutes or longer if you like a deeper shade, then rinse out in cold water. Press ribbons dry with a warm iron.

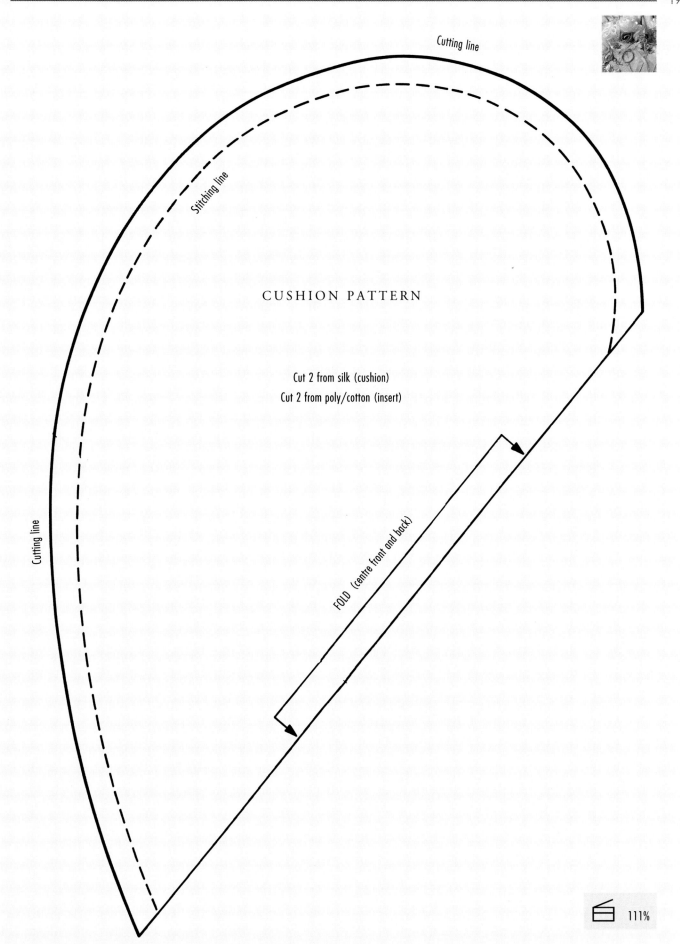

Cutting line

Stitching line

CUSHION PATTERN

Cut 2 from silk (cushion)
Cut 2 from poly/cotton (insert)

Cutting line

FOLD (centre front and back)

111%

PLACEMENT GUIDE

SS

KEY

bud

25mm (1in) cream satin-edged organdy rose and bud

13mm (1/2in) cream tea-dyed rayon ribbon rose

13mm (1/2in) pale gold rayon ribbon rose

8mm (3/8in) cream tea-dyed rayon ribbon rose

7mm (1/4in) cream silk ribbon rose

15mm (5/8in) sheer gold ribbon rose

25mm (1in) sheer olive leaves

Spider's Web Flower Sprays

Bullion Sprays

Cream Pearl Clusters

Seed Bead Clusters

Bouquet of Roses

*Black velvet provides a dramatic background for the delicate
beauty of this ribbon embroidery. Hand-dyed lace,
an antique-style brooch, metallic and silk threads with beads and
diamantes, all add to the opulence of this stunning design.*

Hanah Silk hand-dyed silk ribbons are very delicate and must be handled with care. Use short lengths of ribbon, no more than 30cm (12in) long. Some experience in silk ribbon embroidery is advisable for this project.

When stitching the rosebuds and petals together, use a fine No 8 milliner's needle. Because the Hanah Silks are very delicate, always use the chenille No 13 needle to pull the ribbon through the velvet fabric.

Use a chenille No 18 for the narrower ribbons such as 4mm (⅛in) silk ribbon and the Hanah 15mm (⅝in) width for small buds and centres of roses. Use No 3 milliner's needle for French Knots in the Queen Anne's Lace and gold Bullions of sprays. For all stems and Fly Stitch leaves, use chenille No 22.

PREPARATION

Overlock the edges of the velvet to prevent the pile from shedding. With chalk pencil, mark a cross on the centre of the velvet. Start with a vertical line of 41cm (16in). Measure and mark 18cm (7in) from the top of the line. At this point, mark in the vertical cross line of 35.5cm (14in). You may also choose to chalk around the outline of the cross. This gives you the basic shape of the bouquet.

The actual arrangement of the flowers and which decorative extras such as lace, diamantes and brooch you choose to use is up to you. Study the close-up

photograph for ideas, but use your own creative touch to create an individual work. Position the lace and stitch into place with small stitches.

EMBROIDERY

CABBAGE ROSES

Using 25mm (1in) wide Cherry Blossom and Blushing Bride together, make a Cabbage Rose (see Folded Ribbon Rose page 34), stopping when it is about half the size of a full-blown rose. Stitch to secure. To give the rose its soft, full effect, make individual petals in each of the colours as follows: cut a 14cm (5½in) piece of 35mm (1½in) ribbon. Refer to Diagram 1 on page 24. Fold the corners down at a 90 degree angle and stitch along the bottom with a single strand of matching cotton. Pull up the gathering stitch to create the petal and stitch in place around the rose. Make the next petal in the contrasting colour and stitch onto the rose, half overlapping the previous petal. Keep alternating the two colours, ending with the lighter colour on the outside of the rose.

Continue making a mixture of different coloured roses – Cherry Blossom with Blushing Bride, Cherry Blossom with Victorian Rose, Blushing Bride on its own. Refer to the colour photograph for suggestions of colour combinations. There are two large cabbage roses and three slightly smaller ones. Stitch the large roses in place. These roses will form the basis of the design.

For the buds, make only the folded rose, again using a variety of 25mm (1in) wide ribbons. Match the buds to the full roses. Make some buds with double ribbon, some with single.

FINISHED SIZE

- 41cm x 35.5cm (16in x 14in)

MATERIALS

- 58cm x 52cm (23in x 20½in) black dress velvet
- Antique-style brooch
- Hand-dyed lace pieces
- Hanah silks: 35mm (1½in) wide – 1.5m (1⅝yd) each of Blushing Bride and Cherry Blossom; 25mm (1in) wide – 5m (5½yd) each of Blushing Bride and Cherry Blossom, 4m (4⅜yd) Victorian Rose, 3.5m (3⅞yd) Rose Nectar, 2.5m (2¾yd) Chameleon, 2m (2¼yd) Earth Mother, 1.5m (1⅝yd) Pine Needle; 15mm (⅝in) wide – 4m (4⅜yd) Garnet, 1m (1⅛yd) each of Chameleon and Pine Needle; 11mm (⁷⁄₁₆in) wide 1m (1⅛yd) each of Chameleon and Pine Needle
- YLI silk ribbon: 4mm (⅛in) wide – 2m (2¼yd) each of gold (54) and old gold (52)
- Anchor Stranded Cotton: one skein each of green (263) and brown (339)
- Kacoonda pure silk thread: one packet each of fine variegated olive green (8E) and thick blue/mauve/pink (3)
- Madeira Metallic Thread: gold (5014)
- YLI Fine Metallic Gold Thread
- Sewing threads to match roses
- Delica gold seed beads
- Chenille needles No 13, 18 and 22
- Milliner's needles No 8 and 3
- Chalk pencil

NOTE: this is an inspirational project. Quantities are given as a guide only. Actual colour placement is a matter or personal preference. Although no pattern is given, there is a placement diagram on page 27 for you to follow. This diagram is not full size.

STITCHES USED

Straight Stitch, Ribbon Stitch, Pistil Stitch,
Stem Stitch, Fly Stitch, French Knot,
Bullion Stitch

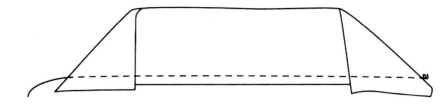

Diagram 1
Cabbage Rose petal

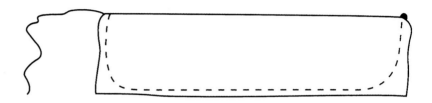

Diagram 2
Open Rose petal

Add Ribbon Stitch leaves around the buds in 15mm (⅝in) or 11mm (⁷⁄₁₆in) green ribbon. Stem Stitch in the stems using two strands of green stranded embroidery cotton. Work lots of leaves around the cabbage roses using the 25mm (1in) wide Chameleon and Earth Mother ribbons.

OPEN ROSES

Using 25mm (1in) wide Rose Nectar ribbon, cut 10cm (4in) lengths for petals – five petals for each rose.

Refer to Diagram 2 above. Gather each petal with a single strand of thread, down one side, along the bottom edge and up the other side, curving around the corners. Trim off the corners before pulling the ribbon up into a gather.

Decide where you want to place the rose and stitch the first petal into position. Add the next four petals, each half overlapping the previous petal and with the first and last petals overlapping. The centre of the rose should only be big enough to fill with a cluster of five or six French Knots in 4mm (⅛in) gold silk ribbon. Work a series of Pistil Stitches in a

single strand of brown embroidery cotton all around the ribbon knots to make a densely filled centre.

Thread a No 13 chenille needle with 25mm (1in) wide Pine Needle ribbon and work Ribbon Stitch leaves around the roses. Add some buds (two Ribbon Stitches close together, with 11mm (⁷⁄₁₆in) Pine Needle Ribbon Stitch leaves either side and small Straight Stitch calyx). If needed, work stems in Stem Stitch with two strands of embroidery cotton.

On the left of the bouquet is a side-view rose looking down (see close-up below). Work five Ribbon Stitch petals in the shape of a fan, add some shorter

petals over the top, stitching through the previous Ribbon Stitches. Soften each petal by pulling the ribbon back after you have pulled it to a point. Add the green leaves in Ribbon Stitch using 11mm (7/16in) Earth Mother ribbon. Pull some of the leaves through the petals of the rose and some facing down towards the stem.

The side-view pale pink rose on the right-hand side of the design (see close-up below) is worked by stitching Ribbon Stitch base petals around a circle. Make the petals different lengths so as to create an uneven effect around the edges. Make another bud as before and stitch down into the centre with matching thread.

SMALL GARNET FLOWERS

Thread 15mm (5/8in) wide Garnet ribbon into No 18 chenille needle. Work five Ribbon Stitch petals in a circle. For the flower centres, add three French Knots using the old gold silk ribbon. Work Ribbon Stitch leaves using 15mm (5/8in) green ribbon.

The buds are two Ribbon Stitches side-by-side using 15mm (5/8in) Garnet ribbon, with a Ribbon Stitch leaf in 11mm (7/16in) green ribbon either side of the bud. Stems are Stem Stitched in two strands of embroidery cotton.

QUEEN ANNE'S LACE

Outline the shape of the stems with a chalk pencil. Thread a No 8 milliner's needle with Kacoonda fine silk thread in variegated olive green and Stem Stitch over the outline. Whip over the Stem Stitching with fine gold metallic YLI thread. The flower heads are five French Knots stitched close together with Kacoonda thick pure silk blue/mauve/pink. Finish with a gold seed bead in the centre of each flower.

FINE GOLD SPRAYS

Draw these in with chalk pencil. Thread a No 8 milliner's needle with fine gold metallic thread. Stitch in the stems using Fly Stitch. On each stem, work a 10-wrap Bullion Stitch using Madeira metallic gold thread. Add a few Fly Stitch leaves in the same metallic thread.

FINISHING

Take a careful look at your piece. If there are empty gaps, fill with more leaves or buds. Glue the brooch in place, stitch a few diamantés or beads onto the lace. Stitch all loose ribbons down at the back of your work. Your bouquet of roses is now ready for framing. Take your work to a professional framer who is experienced in framing needlework.

PLACEMENT DIAGRAM

Lace & Roses Needlework Set

*This very elegant set is something no embroiderer should
be without. It comprises needle book, scissors scabbard, pincushion
and hussif — a handy roll for storing those little sewing
odds and ends that always go astray.*

EMBROIDERY

NOTE: the appropriate point at which to do the embroidery is indicated in the individual instructions for each piece.

Spider's Web Rose

See Stitch Guide p160 to make the rose. The 4mm (⅛in) pink silk ribbon is used for the Fly Stitch and the two extra spokes of the web. Bring the ribbon from the back at the centre of the web and weave around clockwise over and under each spoke until you have been around four times.

Rose Buds

The buds are worked in Ribbon Stitch using 4mm (⅛in) pink ribbon. Stitch eight buds approximately 6mm (¼in) from the rose. See Diagram 1 below.

Diagram 1
Rose and Buds

Leaves and Stems

Using 2mm (¹⁄₁₆in) green ribbon, stitch a Fly Stitch to surround each bud, with the

Diagram 2
Completed design

holding stitch extending back to the rose forming a stem. Add tiny Lazy Daisy leaves. See Diagram 2 below.

PIN CUSHION

Cut a 12cm (4¾in) square of damask and 12cm (4¾in) length of insertion lace. Lay the lace over the centre of the fabric and tack into position. Work the embroidery in the centre of the lace.

Cut batting as follows: 1 x 12cm (4¾in) square, 1 x 10cm (4in) square and 4 x 9cm (3½in) squares. Layer the batting with the smallest pieces on the bottom and the largest piece over the top. Cover the mound of batting with the embroidered damask and pull the sides of the fabric to make a dome shape. Tie with thread to hold securely. Make sure that the top is smooth. Fit into the thimble and push any excess or pleated fabric with the smooth edge of the scissors. Finish with a 7mm (¼in) bow of pink and green ribbon.

FINISHED SIZE

- Pin Cushion: 5cm (2in) high and 10cm (4in) wide
  Needle Book: 6.5cm (2½in) square
  Hussif: 15cm x 27cm (6in x 10½in)
  Scissors Scabbard: 10cm x 7cm (4in x 2¾in)

MATERIALS

- 20cm x 140cm (8in x 56in) white damask
- 1m x 4cm (1⅛yd x 1½in) guipure lace edging
- 50cm x 4cm (20in x 1½in) guipure lace insertion
- 20cm (8in) pellon
- Small piece white linen for needle book pages
- Hand-dyed vintage silk ribbon: 4m x 4mm (4⅜yd x ⅛in) pink, 4m x 2mm (4⅜yd x ¹⁄₁₆in) green and 1.5m x 7mm (1⅝yd x ¼in) of both pink and green
- Piece of white cardboard
- 5cm (2in) tall pewter thimble
- No 22 tapestry needle
- No 9 crewel needle
- 450 craft glue
- 30cm (12in) polyester batting
- 2 x small clear press studs
- Scissors scabbard kit
- Embroidery scissors
- Embroidery hoop

STITCHES USED

Spider's Web Rose,
Ribbon Stitch, Lazy Daisy Stitch,
Fly Stitch, Whip Stitch

NEEDLE BOOK

Cut 2 x 6.5cm (2½in) squares of cardboard. Cut 2 x 6.5cm (2½in) squares of pellon. Cut a piece of damask 18cm x 10.5cm (7in x 4¼in). Glue the pellon onto one side of each cardboard piece.

Cut 2 x 12cm (4¾in) lengths of edging lace and 1 x 12cm (4¾in) piece of insertion lace. With right side of the damask facing up, lay insertion lace into position, centring it on the right hand half of damask. Stitch in place. Lay edging lace into position on either side of the insertion lace, covering the join. Stitch into position. Work the embroidery.

Lay the pellon side of the cardboard onto the wrong side of the damask, leaving lcm (⅜in) space between the cardboard pieces. Turn edges in neatly and glue. Trim away any excess.

Cut a piece of damask 7cm x 1.5cm (2¾in x ⅝in). Fold over a small hem and glue into the space between the cardboard pieces to form the spine.

Cut 2 x 6cm (2⅜in) squares of cardboard and cover one side of each with damask, fold the excess to the back, then glue in place. Glue these covered squares to the wrong side of the needle book cover.

Cut a 12.5cm x 6cm (5in x 2⅜in) piece of linen for the needle book pages and fray the edges. Run a line of glue down the spine of the needle book and press linen into position. Place a piece of pink ribbon down the centre and fold the ends under at top and bottom. Slip stitch the ribbon into place.

Stitch a small clear press stud at the centre of the outer edge and finish the book with a small bow of 7mm (¼in) pink and green ribbon.

HUSSIF

Cut three pieces of damask, 27cm x 15cm (10⅝in x 6in). Fold one piece in half lengthwise and press.

Cut one piece of pellon, 27cm x 15cm (10⅝in x 6in). Cut 2 x 27cm (10⅝in) lengths of edging lace and 1 x 27cm (10⅝in) length of insertion lace.

Centre and stitch the edging lace down one piece of damask. Overlap the edging lace to cover join and stitch in place. Complete your ribbon embroidery 4cm (1½in) from one end.

Layer your fabrics in this order: pellon, damask (right-side up), folded damask (raw edge to raw edge) and damask with lace and embroidery (right-side down).

Stitch using a 6mm (¼in) seam allowance, leaving an opening at one side. Clip across the corners. Turn through to right side and ensure that the corners are turned right out.

Divide into three equal sections and stitch through all layers to create three pockets. Thread the cotton ends into a needle and pull through into the pellon to neaten. With pocket side facing up, fold the right-hand side in and overlap with left-hand side. Stitch a press stud in

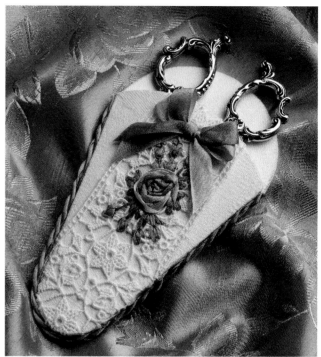

place for closure and finish with a small bow in 7mm (¼in) pink and green ribbon as shown above.

SCISSORS SCABBARD

Cut one piece of damask with 12mm (½in) seam allowance for each piece of cardboard in the scabbard kit. Cut a length of insertion lace for front. Stitch to one of the smaller pieces of damask. Complete the embroidery as shown.

Cover the scabbard pieces, turning over the seam allowance, then glue in place. Join the two backs and two fronts together with a neat Whip Stitch, then join the front to the back, gluing and Whip Stitching.

Make a twisted cord with your remaining lengths of 7mm (¼in) pink and green ribbon and glue over the join.

Finish with a 7mm (¼in) pink and green silk ribbon bow.

 **HELPFUL HINT**

As this project incorporates a number of stitches, it's a good one for beginners.

Start by practising the required stitches as shown in the Stitch Guide (page 160). It is worth practising until you are competent. Use short lengths of ribbon to avoid it becoming thin and flat. The fullness and richness of the ribbon is the effect you want to create.

When working, use a needle large enough to accommodate the ribbon and practise spreading it as you work, so as to show the full face of the fabric when completed.

A Romance of Roses

*A romantic floral design showcasing full-blown roses made
from the delicate pinks of satin-edged organdy ribbon.
The seed pearls and Bullion Stitch sprays combine to create a
delicate background around the bouquet.*

PREPARATION

Hand or machine overcast raw edges of the fabric. Fold the fabric in quarters and finger-press the centre. Mark centre with a pin.

MAKING
THE ROSES

Refer to the placement diagram and key on page 35 and instructions for making the folded ribbon roses on page 34.

Make three large folded roses in pale pink organdy ribbon. Make four deeper pink roses – fold the 25mm (1in) deeper pink ribbon in half lengthwise and begin folding with satin edge upward.

Make five small roses using salmon pink rayon tape and five smaller buds using only two centre winds and one outward diagonal fold.

Attach the centre pale pink rose just above the centre of the fabric. The pale pink roses either side are attached just slightly lower than the centre one. Place the bread dough urn on the fabric to get the right placement of the roses. Continue attaching the ribbon roses, following the placement diagram. Place bread dough urn on fabric again to check the embroidery still fits comfortably around the urn.

Using Straight Stitch, carefully stitch the ribbon roses onto the furnishing fabric, taking care not to crush the ribbon.

When all the ribbon roses have been attached, make six ribbon leaves (see diagram 1 on page 34) and place so raw edges are tucked under the roses.

FINISHED SIZE

- Design Area: 10cm x 8cm (4in x 3¼in)

MATERIALS

- 35cm x 38cm (14in x 15in) pink moiré furnishing fabric
- Handpainted bread dough urn or basket
- 70cm x 15mm (28in x ⅝in) pastel pink Mokuba satin-edged organdy ribbon
- 80cm x 25mm (31½in x 1in) deeper pink Mokuba satin-edged organdy ribbon
- 30cm x 13mm (12in x ½in) grey-green Mokuba rayon tape
- 1.2m x 8mm (1⅜yd x ⅜in) salmon pink Mokuba rayon tape
- YLI Silk Floss: one card each of deep pink (188), pale pink (7)
- DMC Stranded Embroidery Cotton: one skein deep grey-green (3787)
- Pkt cream seed pearls
- No 7 or 8 crewel needle
- Pale pink sewing thread
- 450 craft glue

STITCHES USED

Bullion Stitch, French Knot, Folded Ribbon Roses,

Straight Stitch, Ribbon Leaves

EMBROIDERY

Work Bullion Stitch rose sprays in a single strand of YLI silk floss. The larger roses are three centre 8–9 wrap Bullions in deeper pink, with two 8–9 wrap Bullions in pale pink on either side. The small roses have two 4–5 wrap Bullions in deeper pink, with one 4–5 wrap Bullion in paler pink on either side. Work the French Knots in pale pink at the tip of the Bullion Stitch rose sprays.

Add Straight Stitch leaves (stitched twice into the same holes for added texture) and stems using two strands of deep grey-green stranded cotton.

Stitch seed pearl clusters using a single strand of pink or cream sewing thread to attach pearls.

Finally, attach bread dough urn using only a minimum of glue and taking care not to smear any onto the surrounding backing fabric.

Date and sign your work, then have it framed professionally.

1.

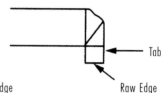

1. Fold ribbon diagonally so a short tab of ribbon comes below the bottom edge.

2. Fold the folded section in half again.

2.

Gather, catching both raw ends

Cut 4cm (1½in) lengths of ribbon. Fold each end forward and slightly down towards the centre. Gather raw edges with running stitch. Stitch securely to backing fabric under the edge of a rose, ensuring all raw edges are hidden.

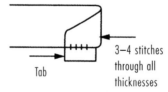

3. Fold entire folded section over again. Stitch in place at base using single sewing thread.

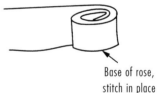

4. Make three more folds, each a little larger than the previous one. Stitch ribbon in place at base of rose through all thicknesses. Stitch sides of base in, to keep a rounded shape.

Diagram 1
Ribbon leaves

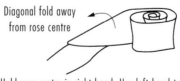

5. Hold rose centre in right hand. Use left hand to fold ribbon in a long diagonal fold away from rose centre. Use right hand to turn rose centre so that diagonal fold wraps about halfway around the rose. Stitch the edge of new ribbon fold to side of rose base.

6. Continue diagonal folding and wrapping until 3–4 wraps have been completed and stitched. After final fold, cut ribbon leaving a short tab. Tuck this end under rose and stitch in place. Leave thread attached to stitch rose to work. Use slip stitches all around the base of the rose, tucking in any raw edges as you stitch. Secure with 3 or 4 stitches on wrong side.

Diagram 2 *Folded Ribbon Rose*

PLACEMENT DIAGRAM

 ss

KEY

 Large pale pink organdy roses

 Larger deeper pink organdy roses

 Salmon pink rayon tape roses and buds, French Knots in floss

 Bullion Stitch rose sprays and French Knots

 Ribbon leaves

 Seed pearl clusters

A Victorian Reticule

*This evening bag, in crushed velvet, is a clever and original design,
displaying a new method for making silk roses that is perfect for wearables.
Creatively decorated with silk ribbons, beads, sequins and pearls, the reticule
is a perfect accessory for a very special occasion.*

PREPARATION

Iron the Whisperweft to the wrong side of the velvet. Using the template given on page 40, cut one large and one small circle from cardboard and one from batting. Cut one rectangle each of velvet and lining fabric, 22cm deep x 70cm wide (8¾in x 27½in). From the remaining velvet and lining, cut a bias strip 5cm (2in) wide across the corner.

Using the cardboard circles as templates, cut one large circle out of the velvet (adding a 1.5cm (⅝in) seam allowance). Then cut one small circle from the lining fabric (adding a 1.5cm (⅝in) seam allowance).

Cut a piece of velvet 10cm x 6cm (4in x 2⅜in) for the hinge. Fold the sides to the centre, overlapping them to give you a piece 10cm x 2.5cm (4in x 1in). Stitch to secure.

Remove the metal screw from the larger (outside) hoop and use pliers to cut away the metal brackets that poke out. The hoop can now be stretched open and closed.

Centre the lace circle on the circle of velvet and machine in place with a small zigzag stitch in matching thread. Using the Placement Guide on page 41 as a reference, lightly mark the position of the three main roses in pencil.

EMBROIDERY

Cover the stitching around the edge of the lace by using a fine needle and sewing thread to catch the grey and dark mauve silk ribbon loosely in place at approximately 7mm (¼in) intervals. Use a small glass bead to cover each stitch. See main photograph.

Refer to the diagram on p38 for the folded ribbon rose specific to this project.

Start by stitching a cluster of glass seed beads across the end of the ribbon at a 45 degree angle.

Fold the ribbon across the glass beads and stitch again at an angle. Continue stitching and folding, making sure that the rose is an irregular shape, not square and boxlike. When you are satisfied with the look of your rose, fold the ribbon under a petal and stitch to secure. Stitch in place on the velvet.

The centre rose was made in Petals rose gold and YLI dusky pink. The roses either side of it were worked in Petals black currant.

For the carnations, take an 8cm (3¼in) length of 13mm (½in) coffee silk ribbon, fold in half lengthwise and run gathering stitches along the fold. Pull up and roll to form the flower. Stitch to secure and stitch in place on the velvet.

The leaves are made from a 6cm (2⅜in) length of green silk ribbon. Fold in half by placing the two cut ends together. Run gathering stitches along the selvedge. Stitch into position on the fabric, pulling the point out to create the leaf shape.

The buds are stitched directly onto the velvet. Work a Detached Chain Stitch in 4mm (⅛in) YLI dark red silk ribbon. Around this, work a large Fly Stitch and then a smaller one in two strands of green DMC.

FINISHED SIZE

- 22cm x 35cm (8½in x 14in)

MATERIALS

- 25cm (10in) silver-grey crushed velvet
- 25cm (10in) satin lining in plum
- 25cm (10in) Whisperweft
- 9cm (3½in) circle of toning lace
- 4mm (⅛in) YLI silk ribbon: 1m (1⅛yd) each of dark red (129) and dark mauve (177), 2m (2¼yd) of grey (29)
- 7mm (¼in) YLI silk ribbon: 1m (1⅛yd) each of green (171) and dusky pink (158)
- Petals 7mm (¼in) silk ribbon in black currant and rose gold
- 13mm (½in) YLI silk ribbon: 20cm (8in) in coffee (57)
- DMC Stranded Embroidery Cotton in green (3346)
- Assorted sequins, pearls, bugle beads and seed beads
- Sewing thread for beading, sewing on leaves and flowers
- Nos 5–10 crewel needles
- No 24 chenille needle
- 1m (1⅛yd) soft cord for handle and edging*
- 10cm (4in) tassel*
- 25cm x 12cm (10in x 4¾in) cardboard
- 25cm x 12cm (10in x 4¾in) batting
- 10cm (4in) wooden embroidery hoop (to frame the lid)
- 450 craft glue
- 2B pencil or tailor's chalk
- Ruler
- Scissors
- Sewing machine

NOTE: *see under Constructing the Bag for materials and quantities for handmade cord and tassel.

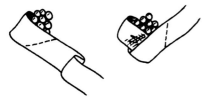

Cover end of ribbon with bead cluster
across a 45 degree angle.

Fold the ribbon across the beads and
stitch at 45 degree angle.

Continue folding and
stitching according to
instructions.

Folded Ribbon Rose

Make the ruffles by gathering a length of 12–15cm (5–6in) grey silk ribbon along the centre, then pulling it up before pinning and stitching into position, trailing through the embroidery.

Add the sequins (stitched on with a bead at the centre), beads and pearls to fill up any spaces in the design. See Placement Guide.

The embroidery should be symmetrical and graduate towards the silk ribbon and bead trim.

CONSTRUCTING THE LID

Lightly glue the large batting onto the large circle of cardboard. Repeat for small circle. Run a gathering stitch by hand around the edge of the embroidered velvet. Place it over the large cardboard and batting, centring the embroidery. Pull the gathering thread firmly. Secure the thread. Repeat the process with lining fabric and small cardboard and batting.

With the outside timber hoop, and starting near the opening in the hoop, fold over the velvet bias strip and tack into position (raw edge to the top). See step-by-step photograph above. Keep the hoop stretched slightly open as you sew so that it will fit comfortably around the inner hoop.

When you have tacked all the way around the hoop, trim away the excess length, fold in the raw edge and stitch to close the overlap. The overlap should be on top of the opening in the wooden hoop so that it will eventually be covered by the fabric hinge.

Repeat the process to cover the inside hoop with the bias cut from the lining fabric. Check that the hoops fit comfortably inside each other.

Place the embroidered circle, right side up, on top of the velvet covered hoop. The centre front of the design should be opposite the seam in the hoop

covering. Fold the raw edges of the bias to the inside. Tuck the narrow end of the fabric hinge between the embroidered circle and the covered hoop, allowing the length to hang down on the outside of the hoop.

Finally, hand sew the embroidered top to the velvet covered hoop with small firm stitches, using two strands of sewing thread for added strength.

Glue the lining covered circle inside the lid. The raw edges should be hidden, with fabric hinge hanging loose.

CONSTRUCTING THE BAG

NOTE: the bag photographed has a hand twisted cord and tassel which is made with blanket stitching over a wooden bead. The thread is YLI Pearl Crown Rayon in colours dusky pink (229), silver/grey (474), and burgundy (245). If you make your own cord and tassel, you will require one reel of each colour.

With the right sides of the velvet together, machine stitch to join the 22cm (8½in) sides. At the base, fold under lcm (⅜in) and tack around with large stitches. Pull the thread to close the opening, pushing the raw edge to the inside. Pull the loop of the tassel through the opening and stitch in place securely.

Using pins, mark the bag top and lining into quarters. Run a gathering thread around the top edge of the bag, then pull the thread to approximately the circumference of the lining covered hoop. Repeat the process for the lining (omitting the tassel).

Mark the quarter points on the lining covered hoop. With the velvet inside out, place the hoop inside the top edge, matching the quarter markings. Place the hinged top so it is at the seam join on the hoop.

Adjust the hinge to allow for easy opening and closing. If necessary, trim off any excess length.

Cut a 45cm (18in) length of cord for the handle (wrap the ends with thread to prevent unravelling). See Placement Guide for position of handles. Attach the cord on either side under the hoop as you stitch the velvet in place.

The cord is also stitched around the lid, starting under the hinge, going around and back under the hinge again. Catch the hinge over the cord so it looks tidy.

With the seams together and the top edge of the lining folded under, Slip Stitch the lining into position. The interior of the bag should look very tidy, with no raw edges. See diagram for position of hinge, button and handles.

Stitch on a decorative button at the centre front of the bag. Make a loop covered with Buttonhole Stitch at the centre front of the lid, big enough to open and close the bag comfortably.

STITCHES USED

Folded Ribbon Rose,

Detached Chain Stitch (Lazy Daisy Stitch),

Fly Stitch, Slip Stitch, Buttonhole Stitch

Cut 1 lace circle

SMALL CIRCLE FOR LINING

Cut 1 cardboard same size

Cut 1 wadding same size

Cut 1 lining with 1.5cm (⅝in) seam allowance

LARGE CIRCLE FOR TOP

Cut 1 cardboard same size

Cut 1 wadding same size

Cut 1 velvet with 1.5cm (⅝in) seam allowance

SS

PLACEMENT GUIDE

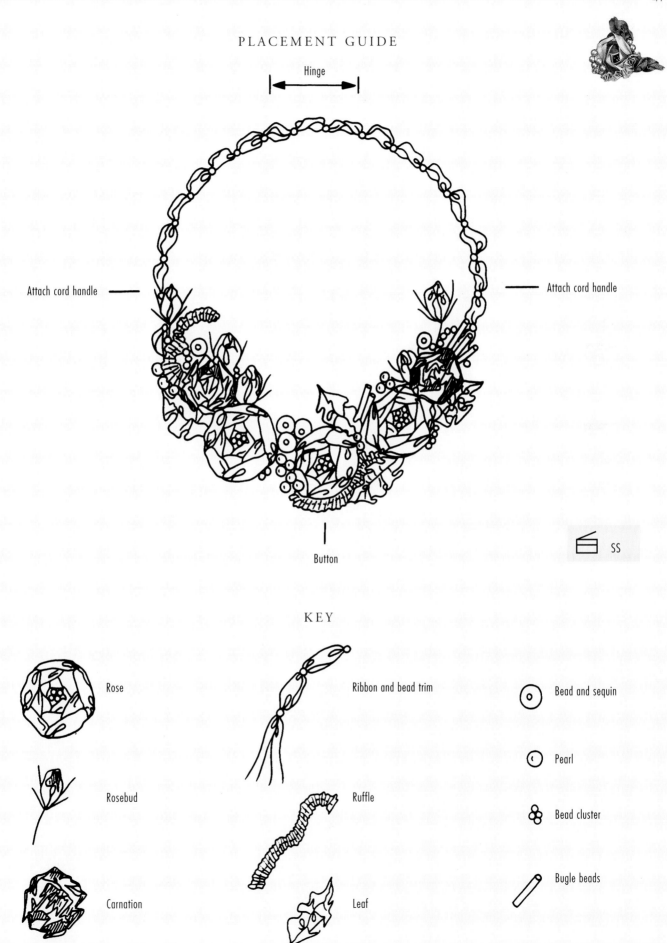

Hinge

Attach cord handle

Attach cord handle

Button

SS

KEY

Rose

Rosebud

Carnation

Ribbon and bead trim

Ruffle

Leaf

Bead and sequin

Pearl

Bead cluster

Bugle beads

Roses for Ellen

*The soft pastels of the ribbon and surface stitches
are entirely worked in — and on — silk,
creating an exquisite embroidery any craftsperson
would be proud of.*

PREPARATION

Trace the design outline onto the fabric using a soft lead pencil. You can do this either by using a light box, or taping the tracing and fabric onto a sunlit window and copying the design.

Use Fray Stoppa or overcast the edges of the fabric to prevent fraying.

EMBROIDERY

NOTE: all the silk thread embroidery is worked with a single strand throughout. Diagrams on page 45 show the order for completing stitching.

Using the No 10 crewel needle and one strand of dark gold silk, commence embroidering the basket in Satin Stitch following the Basket Embroidery Guide. Change to medium gold and embroider the remaining squares in the opposite direction. Using Satin Stitch, embroider the basket handle in dark gold (see photograph on the right for area to be embroidered).

Using silk ribbon and tapestry needle, commence working the five larger roses, three in light dusky pink and two in medium dusky pink. In a single strand of thread to match the ribbon, work five spokes as shown in Spoke Rose diagram on page 45.

Using ribbon, work three French Knots (one twist around the needle) in the centre of the spokes. Come up on the left side of any spoke and commence weaving the ribbon over and under the spokes alternately, lightly twisting the ribbon as you go. Take the ribbon to the back of the work and stitch down with thread to avoid unravelling.

Using medium green ribbon, work the leaves in Ribbon Stitch, then secure at the back of the work.

With ribbon, work the mauve flowers in Ribbon Stitch also. Stitch the central petal first, with a stitch either side at a slight angle. Change to dark gold thread and embroider three French Knots (two twists around the needle) in the centre.

Using lemon ribbon, work lemon single roses with five French Knots (one twist around the needle) close together in a circle. Using dark gold thread, embroider one French Knot (three twists around the needle) in the centre of each flower. Finish off at the back as before.

With light and medium dusky pink ribbon, work half flowers in Ribbon Stitch – only 2–3 petals. Finish off at the back by stitching ribbon down with thread.

Using the straw needle and medium blue silk thread, embroider the forget-me-nots in five French Knots (two twists) in a close circle. Place a gold French Knot (two twists) in the centre.

DESIGN SIZE

- 6.5cm x 8.5cm (2½in x 3¼in)

MATERIALS

- 20cm (8in) square dupion silk
- No 10 straw needle
- No 10 crewel needle
- No 22 tapestry needle
- Madeira Silk thread: one skein each of medium gold (2209), dark gold (2210), pale blue (1104), medium blue (1710), dark blue (1711), pale green (1701), medium green (1703), lemon (0112), medium pink (0813), medium mauve (0807), pale pink (0815), black
- YLI 4mm (⅛in) silk ribbon: medium green (32), medium lemon (13), medium mauve (178), medium dusty pink (158), light dusty pink (157)

Step by step photo of stitch direction

STITCHES USED

Satin Stitch, French Knot, Ribbon Stitch,

Bullion Stitch, Fly Stitch, Lazy Daisy Stitch,

Long and Short Stitch

Work the forget-me-nots close to the ribbon flowers (after a while you will end up working French Knots at random in blue and gold and will not always be able to fit in a perfect five knot flower). The forget-me-not seed pods are worked in French Knots (one twist).

With straw needle and medium pink thread, embroider single Bullion Rose Buds around the outer edge of the design (approximately 3mm (⅛in) Bullions). Work a Fly Stitch around the bud in medium green thread.

With pale green silk thread in a crewel needle, work leaves in tiny Lazy Daisy stitches around the outer edge.

Finally, to add a few flowers on the basket, randomly embroider some French Knots (one twist) in pinks, lemons, mauves and greens to fill in any open spaces.

Using the crewel needle and silk thread, embroider the birds in Long and Short Stitch. Note the Thread Embroidery Guide and step-by-step photo for stitch direction. Three shades of blue are used to shade and shape the bird. Follow diagram and blend the shades together by overlapping stitches.

Do not aim to keep your Satin Stitch soft, smooth and flat. The birds are meant to be fluffed up, so keep your stitches a little loose to achieve this effect.

Using one strand of black, place a French Knot (two twists) for the birds' eyes. For the beak, use dark gold and work two Straight Stitches.

For pink Bullion Roses between the birds, use a straw needle and commence work with medium pink. Work three Bullions approximately 4mm (⅛in) for the centre. Change to pale pink and work a Bullion each side of centre. Continue in the same shade and work another Bullion each side of the above. Place a Bullion across the base of the rose, remembering to add a few extra twists around the needle to make a gentle curve.

Using medium pink, place a Bullion bud each side, following the earlier rose bud directions.

Using medium green, work three leaves each side of the roses. Work one 4mm (⅛in) Bullion Stitch and then place another underneath, a little smaller.

Fill the space between the roses with five French Knots (two twists) in lemon, around a dark gold French Knot (two twists) centre.

Sign and date your embroidery. Professionally framed, you will have an heirloom to give pleasure for many years.

 HELPFUL HINT

To begin embroidery, secure the ribbon at the start with a small backstitch. To secure the end, weave the ribbon behind the stitching.

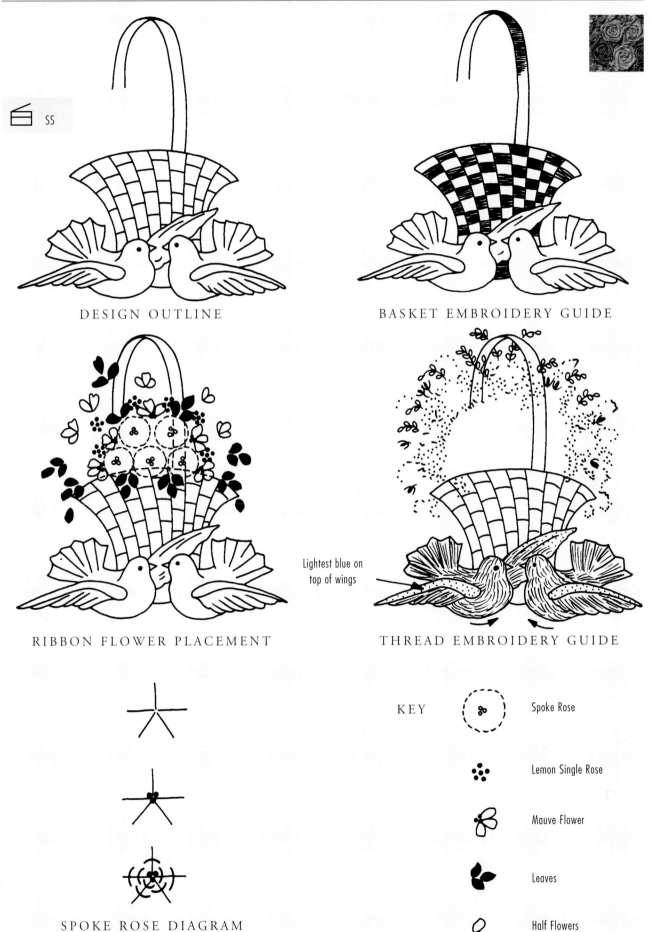

SS

DESIGN OUTLINE

BASKET EMBROIDERY GUIDE

RIBBON FLOWER PLACEMENT

Lightest blue on
top of wings

THREAD EMBROIDERY GUIDE

SPOKE ROSE DIAGRAM

KEY

Spoke Rose

Lemon Single Rose

Mauve Flower

Leaves

Half Flowers

Cottage Garden Embroidery

The beauty of this project is that no two embroiderers will create quite the same garden, and although the instructions will help you recreate the pattern, they are intended as a guide from which you can create your own piece.

DESIGN SIZE

- 20cm x 18cm (8in x 7in)

MATERIALS

- 40cm (16in) Dupion silk
- Embroidery threads (see table)
- YLI silk ribbon (see note and table)
- No 5 and 7 milliner's or straw needles
- No 18, 20 and 22 chenille needles
- Jo Sonja's Artists' Acrylics (optional)
- Bread dough urn
- Brass pedestal and butterfly
- Fine black felt tipped pen
- 2H pencil
- Tracing paper

NOTE: this is an inspirational project and the instructions are given as a guide only. The table indicates stitches, needles, colours and ribbon or thread used. You can follow these closely or do your own interpretation and substitute other materials. You may choose to add a painted background, but this is a matter of personal choice.

The silk ribbon quantities are given only as an estimate. You will require 1m x 4mm (1⅛yd x ⅛in) ribbon in cols 3, 22, 112, 85, 15, 118, 179, 14 and 24. 2m x 4mm (2¼yd x ⅛in) ribbon in cols 54, 21, 125, 44, 8, 32, 112 and 114. 3m x 4mm (3¼yd x ⅛in) ribbon in col 102. 5m x 4mm (5½yd x ⅛in) ribbon in cols 117 and 20. 1m x 7mm (1⅛yd x ¼in) ribbon in col 72. 2m x 7mm (2¼yd x ¼in) silk ribbon in col 8. 1.5m (1⅝yd) x Mokuba ribbon 1542 in col 16

STITCHES USED

Bullion Stitch, Back Stitch, Lazy Daisy Stitch,
French Knot, Buttonhole, Stem Stitch,
Satin Stitch, Pistil Stitch, Ribbon Stitch,
Looped Ribbon Stitch, Folded Roses,
Straight Stitch

PREPARATION

Place the tracing paper over the colour photograph on page 49 and using the felt tipped pen, trace the arbour, stepping stones, hollyhocks and climbing rose stems, and positions of the groups of flowers. Note the arrows on the photograph at the hollyhocks on the left and the foxgloves on the right. Transfer these arrows to your tracing. You will need these marks to determine the enlargement. Using a photocopier, enlarge tracing to measure 20cm (8in) from arrow to arrow. Sticky tape the photocopy onto a light box (or into a sunlit window). Tape your fabric over the tracing and transfer the design to the fabric using the 2H pencil. The pencil lines should be very fine, just enough to see. All pencil lines should be covered with embroidery as work cannot be washed to remove marks.

✂ HELPFUL HINT

Using a hoop is not essential but it can make it easier to hold the work and control tension — particularly if you tend to pull your thread too tight.

BODY

First Bullion – 2 wraps in black

Second Bullion – 4 wraps in yellow

Third Bullion – 5 wraps in black

Fourth Bullion – 4 wraps in yellow

Fifth Bullion – 2 wraps in black

EMBROIDERY

Refer to the table on p50 for instructions for each flower group.

Back Stitch the arbour outline. Stitch the stems for the climbing rose. Sew in Bullion roses and buds, then fill in with Lazy Daisy Stitch leaves.

In freehand, draw the stems winding around the arbour on the opposite side, and stitch. Embroider the wisteria flowers, then fill the gaps with leaves.

Stitch the hollyhock stems, making sure to add French Knots for buds at the top of the stems. Add the flowers and buds, then the leaves under each flower head, working larger leaves around the bottom of the stem.

Draw in the foxglove stems. Stitch the foxglove flowers making sure to taper to the top. Sew in the stems, starting from the top, adding a French Knot under each flower as you join the flower heads running down the stem. Work Ribbon Stitch leaves. Add a single stitch in thread up the middle of the leaves.

Place the pedestal and urn on your fabric and mark their positions. Set pedestal and urn aside. Make 12 folded roses (see p34). Stitch into place. Add leaves and buds and sew the stems for the buds in thread.

Embroider the shasta daisy flowers, then add stems and leaves.

The violets are worked in two Ribbon Stitch petals at the top and three below. Add the centre with a single French Knot. Stitch the stems and leaves.

Draw the stems in place for the delphiniums, stitch the flowers, making them smaller as you stitch to the top of the flower. With a single strand of thread, add a French Knot over the larger Looped Ribbon Stitch (work as for Ribbon Stitch, but pierce the ribbon with the point of the needle, then take the needle through the fabric close to starting point, forming a loop).

Stitch in the grape hyacinths.

The outline of the stepping stones is stitched next, then the yellow daisies and the leaves. Fill in any gaps with petunias, iris, daffodils and alyssum. Refer to the photograph.

Stitch in the ferns and diosma bushes. Stitch a few horizontal Straight Stitches underneath the ferns and some Lazy Daisy leaves spreading out from the base of the diosmas.

Stitch the spider's web and spider. If necessary, fill in any empty spaces with clusters of French Knots and Lazy Daisy Stitch leaves.

PAINTING BACKGROUND

This step is optional. With Jo Sonja's paints, watered down, paint the background, shadowing the flowers, leaves and stepping stones. Add little tufts of grass to soften the foreground.

 130%

FINISHING

Finally, attach the pedestal and urn using only a minimum amount of glue and taking care not to smear any onto the surrounding backing fabric. Sign and date your embroidery, then have it professionaly framed by a framer used to working with fabrics.

Note: When the photograph is increased by 130% the distance between the arrows will measure 20cm (8in) – the correct size for the project.

SUBJECT	STITCH	THREAD	NEEDLE
Arbour	Back Stitch	Edmar Glory dark green (110)	Milliner's No 7
Rose Stems	Back Stitch	Divine Delta light brown (9)	Milliner's No 7
Roses	Bullion	Marlitt pale gold, 1 strand	Milliner's No 5
Rose Leaves	Lazy Daisy	Anchor dark olive, 2 strands	Milliner's No 5
Wisteria	French Knot 2 twists, tapering to 1	4mm (1/8in) silk ribbon purple (102) and dark lavender (117)	Chenille No 20
Leaves	Lazy Daisy	Anchor olive (844), Marlitt olive (1011), 2 strands	Milliner's No 5
Hollyhocks	Buttonhole	Anchor Pink (36) 2 strands, Divine Delta very dark pink (9)	Milliner's No 5 Milliner's No 7
Stems	Stem Stitch	Edmar Glory dark green (110)	Milliner's No 5
Leaves	Satin Stitch	Edmar Glory dark green (110)	Milliner's No 5
Centres	French Knot	Anchor light orange (311), 2 strands	Chenille No 22
Shasta Daisies	Lazy Daisy	Anchor soft white (2), 2 strands	Milliner's No 5
Centres	French Knot	Anchor orange (303), 2 strands	Milliner's No 5
Leaves	Ribbon Stitch	4mm (1/8in) silk ribbon dark green (21)	Chenille No 20
Delphinium	Looped Ribbon Stitch	4mm (1/8in) silk ribbon blue (125) and deeper blue (44)	Chenille No 20
Centres	French Knot	Marlitt green (1011) 1 strand	Milliner's No 5
Leaves	Ribbon Stitch	4mm (1/8in) silk ribbon leaf green (20)	Chenille No 20
Roses in Urn	Hand made folded ribbon roses	7mm (1/4in) silk ribbon pink (8)	Milliner's No 7
Buds	Ribbon Stitch	4mm (1/8in) silk ribbon pink (8) and deep pink (24)	Chenille No 20
Leaves	Lazy Daisy	4mm (1/8in) silk ribbon green (32)	Chenille No 20
Foxgloves	Looped Ribbon Stitch	4mm (1/8in) silk ribbon medium pink (112) and deepest pink (114)	Chenille No 20
Stems	Straight Stitch with a French Knot under Flower	Edmar Glory dark green (110)	Milliner's No 5
Leaves	Ribbon Stitch with Straight Stitch in thread	7mm (1/4in) silk ribbon dark green (72)	Chenille No 18
Violets	Ribbon Stitch	4mm (1/8in) silk ribbon purple (85)	Chenille No 18

SUBJECT	STITCH	THREAD	NEEDLE
Centres	French Knot	4mm (1/8in) silk ribbon bright yellow (15)	Chenille No 22
Leaves	Buttonhole	Anchor green (263), 1 strand	Milliner's No 5
Grape Hyacinths	French Knot	4mm (1/8in) silk ribbon deep lavender (117)	Chenille No 20
Stems	Straight Stitch	Anchor green (263), 2 strands	Milliner's No 5
Petunias	Buttonhole	Anchor purple (101) and deep pink (63), 2 strands	Milliner's No 5
Yellow Daisy	Lazy Daisy	Anchor bright yellow (303), 2 strands	Milliner's No 5
Centre	French Knot	Anchor tan (884), 1 strand	Milliner's No 5
Leaves	Lazy Daisy	Edmar Glory dark green (110)	Milliner's No 5
Iris	Lazy Daisy and Straight Stitch	4mm (1/8in) silk ribbon deepest lavender (118) and dusty mauve (179)	Chenille No 18
Centre	Small Straight Stitch	4mm (1/8in) silk ribbon gold (54)	Chenille No 22
Leaves	Ribbon Stitch	4mm (1/8in) silk ribbon leaf green (20)	Chenille No 20
Daffodil	Ribbon Stitch	4mm (1/8in) silk ribbon yellow (14)	Chenille No 20
Trumpet	2 Ribbon Stitches not pulled tight	4mm (1/8in) silk ribbon gold (54)	Chenille No 20
Stems	Stem Stitch	Anchor green (844), 1 strand	Milliner's No 5
Leaves	Ribbon Stitch	4mm (1/8in) silk ribbon leaf green (20)	Chenille No 20
Alyssum	French Knot	4mm (1/8in) silk ribbon white (3), mauve (22), rose pink (112)	Chenille No 20
Leaves	Lazy Daisy	Anchor in a different green for each flower colour, 2 strands	Milliner's No 5
Diosma	French Knot	Marlitt palest mauve (1214), 2 strands	Milliner's No 5
Stems	Straight Stitch	Edmar Glory dark green (110)	Milliner's No 5
Fern	Ribbon Stitch	Mokuba Ribbon 1542 (col No 16)	Chenille No 20
Stepping Stones	Back Stitch	Divine Deltalt brown (9)	Milliner's No 5
Bees	Bullion Stitch body, and Pistil Stitch antennae	Anchor black and bright yellow (303), 1 strand	Milliner's No 7
Wings	Lazy Daisy	Gold Metallic, 1 strand	Milliner's No 5
Spider's Web	Straight Stitch, whipped around	Gold Metallic, 1 strand	Milliner's No 5
Spider	French Knot body, Straight Stitch legs	Anchor black, 1 strand	Milliner's No 5

Bouquet of Pastel Favourites

A bunch of the best-loved cottage garden flowers
is embroidered on this elegant lap rug,
complemented by subtly shaded silk ribbons,
pure silk and rayon threads.

PREPARATION

Using a pencil, trace the main design from the pattern sheet onto a large piece of voile lining. Fold the blanketing in half vertically and horizontally to find the centre. Tack the voile to the wrong side of the blanket (the fluffy side is the right side), centring the design.

Mark the stems with running stitch in contrasting machine thread, working from the back. Mark the outlines of the main flowers in the same way. The corner motifs are traced on page 57 and transferred in the same way, positioned 6cm (2³⁄₈in) in from each corner.

EMBROIDERY

NOTE: do not split the silk thread, work with all strands.

STEMS

Working from the front, using the chenille needle and green silk thread, work Chain Stitch along each stem. Start each stem at the base and make large stitches.

LEAVES

Stitch the small leaves in Lazy Daisy using green silk thread. The large leaves are worked in slightly spaced Satin Stitch with a relaxed tension. See photograph.

FORGET-ME-NOTS

These are worked in Straight Stitch using pale blue ribbon. Work between eight and 12 stitches per flower, twisting the ribbon occasionally. Stitch from the outside into the middle. Add some Straight Stitches in cream floss to a few flowers. See photograph.

MARGUERITES

Using apricot ribbon, work in Lazy Daisy Stitch. To vary the effect, alternate long stitches and short stitches.

DAISIES

Chain Stitch the central circle with lemon floss. Space about ten pale pink 4mm (¹⁄₈in) ribbon petals in Lazy Daisy around this centre.

ZINNIAS

The centre of the flower is worked in Satin Stitch using white floss. Work about ten Straight Stitch petals around the centre using 7mm (¹⁄₄in) pink ribbon. See photograph below.

FINISHED SIZE

- 80cm x 100cm (31¹⁄₂in x 39in)

MATERIALS

- 80cm x 100cm (31¹⁄₂in x 39in) blush coloured pure wool blanketing
- 80cm x 100cm (31¹⁄₂in x 39in) fabric for backing
- Cotton voile lining for the embroidery
- 4.5m (4⁷⁄₈yd) blanket binding
- Machine thread in contrasting colour to blanketing
- 4mm (¹⁄₈in) YLI silk ribbon: 6m (6⁵⁄₈yd) pale pink (5), 2m (2¹⁄₄yd) mid-pink (157), 4m (4³⁄₈yd) apricot (166), 6m (6⁵⁄₈yd) pale blue (97) and 3m (3¹⁄₄yd) lemon (13)
- 7mm (¹⁄₄in) YLI silk ribbon: 2m (2³⁄₈yd) pink (5) and 1m (1¹⁄₈yd) cream (156)
- 32mm (1¹⁄₄in) YLI silk ribbon: 1m (1¹⁄₈yd) cream (156), 3m (3¹⁄₄yd) each of white (1) and pink (5)
- Rayon ribbon floss in lemon and white
- 2 pkts Au Ver á Soie – Soie d'Alger green silk thread (2111)
- No 8 chenille needle
- No 20 crewel needle for roses and hollyhocks
- Pencil

NOTE: see pattern sheet for main design

STITCHES USED

Chain Stitch, Straight Stitch, Lazy Daisy Stitch, Satin Stitch, French Knot

Zinnias and Forget-Me-Nots

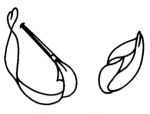

Making twisted loops

Work loops around the centre

Diagram 1
Asters

Securing tube and folding ribbon

Gathering ribbon

Completed rose

Diagram 2
Gathered Roses

Asters and Forget-Me-Nots

ASTERS

See Diagram 1. Using 4mm (⅛in) mid-pink ribbon, work a row of twisted loops around a 1cm (⅜in) diameter circle. Work another row of twisted loops just inside these, using pale pink ribbon, then work a circle of yellow French Knots inside the loop petals.

ROSES

See Diagram 2 left. Cut a 30cm(12in)strip of 32mm (1¼in) white silk ribbon and another of pink silk ribbon. Place the pink ribbon on the white ribbon and fold in half lengthwise with the pink on the inside. Fold in 6mm (¼in) on the short end and roll 2cm (¾in) of ribbon towards you to form a tube, stitching to secure it with matching thread, one third of the way up the tube. Fold the ribbon forward on the diagonal and turn. Stitch in place. Fold forward, turn and stitch. Fold forward, turn and stitch. Fold, turn

and stitch once more. Now the selvedges should be uppermost on the rose. With a running stitch, gather the remainder of the ribbon on the lower folded edge and

Roses

Gathering ribbon

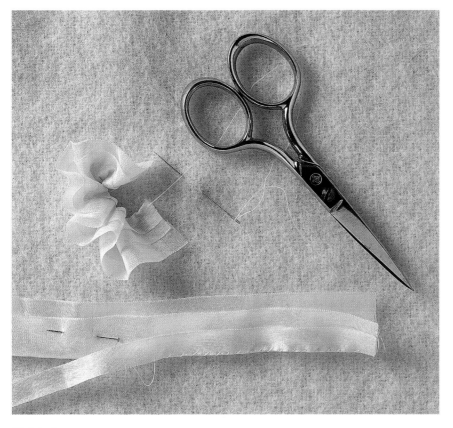

Hollyhocks

Completed hollyhock

Diagram 3
Large Hollyhocks

stitch to the base. Fold the raw edge down diagonally. Stitch the rose to the blanketing. Bring the needle up through the base of the petals three or four times to attach.

LARGE HOLLYHOCKS

See Diagram 3. Cut 20cm (8in) of 32mm (1¼in) cream ribbon. Fold lengthwise with one edge a little higher than the other. Cut 20cm (8in) of 7mm (¼in) pink ribbon and lay this over the short edge of the cream ribbon. Run a row

of gathering stitches along the base of the ribbon and pull up to form the flower. Secure with a few small stitches at the base and attach to the blanketing with matching thread.

SMALL HOLLYHOCKS

As above, using 20cm (8in) of 7mm (¼in) cream ribbon (do not fold) with 20cm (8in) pale pink ribbon.

When all embroidery has been completed, remove any tacking threads and trim excess voile from the back.

HELPFUL HINT

This is a perfect project in which to dabble with your own colour combinations. Allow yourself plenty of time to experiment with colours and practise new stitches, swapping and adapting to add your own personal touch. The more time you spend on preparation, the more likely you are to enjoy your working time and the finished result. Don't be alarmed by the appearance of the back of the work, as this will be covered with backing fabric.

MAKING UP

Tack blanket lining to the back of your lap rug. Trim edges to neaten if necessary. Press under a 6mm (¼in) seam on both edges of the binding. Open binding and place on blanketing, right sides together and raw edges even. Hand or machine stitch the binding to the blanket, mitring the corners. Turn binding to the back and slip stitch along the pressed seam.

CORNER DESIGNS

TOP LEFT

Marguerite

Forget-me nots
(pale blue ribbon)

BOTTOM LEFT

Aster

TOP RIGHT

Lazy Daisy leaves
(green silk thread)

Zinnia

BOTTOM RIGHT

French Knots
(lemon ribbon)

Rose

143%

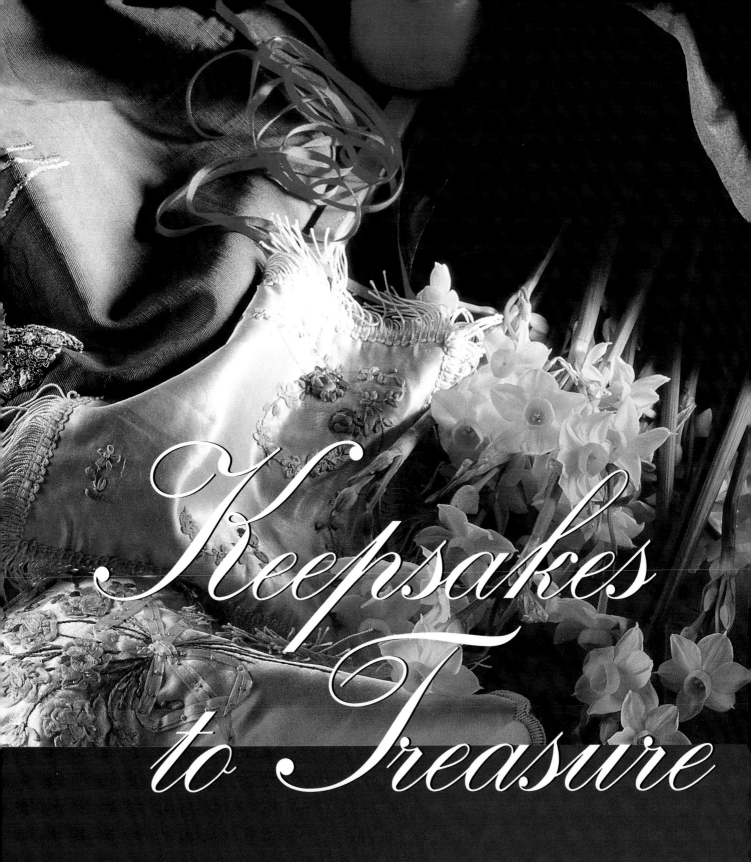

Keepsakes
to Treasure

*A keepsake is a token of remembrance that expresses
a special part of us and as such is to be valued,
put on display or given to a special family
member or friend.*

Tudor Garden

*This charming ribbon-embroidered garden is a delightful
compilation of five of the best-loved garden flowers.
Once added to your repertoire, these flowers can be used individually
or incorporated into many different designs.*

PREPARATION

If your fabric has a tendency to fray, over-lock or hand overcast the edges. Trace and transfer the design on page 63 onto the fabric by your preferred method. You will probably only need to transfer the inner and outer borders as the design can be successfully worked freehand. Refer to the close-up colour photograph.

EMBROIDERY

OUTER BORDERS

Work two rows of Chain Stitch in varie-gated green Perlé. Outside this border, work a row of French Knots in dark blue-green Perlé.

INNER BORDERS

Work the diamond border of Chain Stitch with variegated green Perlé.

stranded cotton. The leaves at the base of the plants are Ribbon Stitched in 7mm (¼in) yellow green ribbon.

LAVENDER

Work the stems in Straight Stitch with green Perlé. Form the base of the flowers by working seven French Knots very close together with dark purple 4mm (⅛in) silk ribbon. Complete the flowers by working Ribbon Stitches at the top of each cluster of French Knots, using the purple 4mm (⅛in) silk ribbon.

DESIGN AREA

- 17cm (6¾in) square

MATERIALS

- 35cm (14in) square linen or preferred background fabric
- DMC Coton Perlé No 5: one skein each of variegated green (122) and green (987)
- DMC Coton Perlé No 3: one skein dark blue-green (924)
- DMC Stranded Embroidery Cotton: one skein each of green (3364) and yellow (725)
- 4mm (⅛in) YLI silk ribbon: 2m (2¼yd) each of blue (98), purple (102) and dark purple (85)
- 7mm (¼in) YLI silk ribbon: 2m (2¼yd) each of light green (31), soft apricot (135), 1m (1⅛yd) each of orange (40), yellow (15), apricot (167), light pink (111), pink (24), deep pink (146), green (33), yellow-green (20)
- No 6 crewel needle for stranded cotton
- No 3 crewel needle for Coton Perlé
- No 18 chenille needle for silk ribbon

STITCHES USED

Ribbon Stitch, French Knot,

Chain Stitch, Lazy Daisy Stitch,

Straight Stitch, Gathered Rose

FORGET-ME-NOTS

The flower is formed by Straight Stitches with 4mm (⅛in) blue silk ribbon. Complete the flower by working a single-wrap French Knot with two strands of yel-low cotton in the centre. The Straight Stitch stems and small Lazy Daisy leaves are worked with two strands of green

DAFFODILS

The stems are Straight Stitched in green Perlé. The buds and top petals of the flowers are worked in Straight Stitches with 7mm (¼in) yellow silk ribbon. The trumpet is formed by a Ribbon Stitch using the orange 7mm (¼in) silk ribbon.

FOXGLOVES

Work the stem of each plant with a Straight Stitch in green Perlé. Use the three shades of 7mm (¼in) pink for the flowers, working the two smaller plants in light pink and one each of the larger plants in pink and deep pink. Form the base of the plant with Ribbon Stitches. Work the buds at the top of the plants with Straight Stitches. Add the greenery of the buds in small Straight Stitches with the green Perlé and the leaves of the bud in Ribbon Stitch using the green silk ribbon.

ROSE AND
ROSEBUDS

Work the rosebuds in Ribbon Stitch with 7mm (¼in) soft apricot silk ribbon. Work the greenery around each bud with Straight Stitches in the green Perlé. Add the Ribbon Stitch leaves in light green 7mm (¼in) silk ribbon.

Finally, make the gathered rose for the centre of the design. See diagram page 54. Cut 30cm (12in) each of the apricot and soft apricot 7mm (¼in) silk ribbon. Place the two ribbons on top of each other and sew them together with a running stitch along a selvedge. Gather and sew to the fabric with small stitches until you have the effect you wish to create.

 HELPFUL HINT

This is an ideal beginner's project because it incorporates all the basic steps for embroidery and silk ribbon embroidery.

Start by practising the stitches as illustrated in the Stitch Guide on page 160. Practise until you are competent. Be careful not to overwork the ribbon or it will become thin and flat. You really want to create a look of fullness and richess. Work with short pieces of ribbon no longer than 50cm (20in) and use a needle with an eye large enough to accommodate the ribbon. In particular, practise spreading the ribbon to show the full face of the fabric when the embroidery is completed.

EMBROIDERY DESIGN

KEY

→	Ribbon Stitch
↰	Straight Stitch
○●	French Knot
A	Forget-me-nots
B	Lavender
C	Rose and Rosebuds
D	Daffodils
E	Foxgloves

 SS

The Essence of Spring

*Spring blossoms are in rich profusion on this
silk embroidered cushion. This project will inspire you
to create your own bouquet of delicate flowers
to bloom throughout the year.*

EMBROIDERY

Cut a 43cm (17in) square for the cushion front. With a fabric pencil, mark the placement of the larger roses. After working the roses and buds, draw in the stems, bringing them down through the position where the bow will be tied. Work stems in Stem Stitch, before adding the leaves.

Repeat these steps for the smaller roses. Work the chrysanthemums, then the daisies, making sure to draw in all stems and buds after you have worked the flower heads.

Draw in the stems for the shrub flower spray and the lavender, then work the flower heads. Add a few small forget-me-not flowers if there is room (Ribbon Stitch for the petals with a French Knot in the centre).

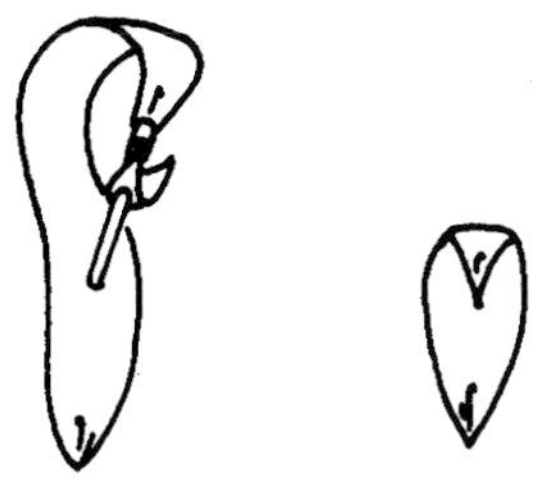

Ribbon Stitch

When the posy is complete, tie a large double bow with 32mm (1 1/2in) silk ribbon (178 and 158). You might choose to touch up some of the flowers and leaves with a little fabric paint if you wish to give them greater depth.

LARGE ROSES

Thread a No 18 chenille needle with 13mm (1/2in) silk ribbon (5). Work eight or nine petals in a loose side Ribbon Stitch in a shape a little like spiders' legs. With 13mm (1/2in) (5) and 7mm (1/4in) (8) ribbon, make a centre bud by working the two ribbons together, keeping the 7mm (1/4in) at the top of the 13mm (1/2in) ribbon. See page 34. Fold the raw edge down a little, then roll the ribbon three or four times to form the centre of the bud. At the bottom of the roll, catch with three or four stitches to secure. Make a petal by folding the ribbon back on the cross. Repeat to make a second petal. To finish off, stitch the ribbon on the bottom of the rose so you will not have any frayed edges. When the centre bud is made, stitch it in place over the petals you have already worked, making sure it is facing the right way.

Add a few more petals with 13mm (1/2in) ribbon (5), using a No 18 chenille needle. Place them around the centre bud. You might also add some petals in 13mm (1/2in) Spark Organdy (3).

The single buds are worked with the 13mm (1/2in) silk ribbon and the Spark Organdy together in one needle. Stitch two or three overlapping Ribbon Stitches, making the back stitch longer than the front. The leaves are worked in Ribbon Stitch using 13mm (1/2in) ribbon (32), while 7mm (1/4in) ribbon (32) is worked around the single rosebuds.

SPIDER ROSE

Thread a No 18 chenille needle with 7mm (1/4in) ribbon (5). Work eight or nine petals in a loose side Ribbon Stitch, in the same manner as the large rose. With the 4mm (1/8in) ribbon (8) add a Ribbon Stitch petal in between each exist-

DESIGN AREA

- 32cm (12 1/2in) square

MATERIALS

- For cushion face: 50cm (20in) Dupion silk fabric (plus if desired, 1m (1 1/8yd) same colour for first frill and 2m (2 1/4yd) contrast colour for second frill and cushion back)
- For large roses: YLI silk ribbon 4m x 13mm (4 3/8yd x 1/2in) (5); 2m x 7mm (2 1/4yd x 1/4in) (8); 2m x 13mm (2 1/4yd x 1/2in) (32); 2m x 7mm (2 1/4yd x 1/4in) (32); 2m x 13mm (2 1/4yd x 1/2in) Spark Organdy (3)
- For spider roses: YLI silk ribbon 4m x 7mm (4 3/4yd x 1/4in) (5); 3m x 4mm (3 1/4yd x 1/8in) (8); 2m x 4mm (2 1/4yd x 1/8in) (158); 3m x 7mm (3 1/4yd x 1/4in) (62)
- For chrysanthemums: YLI 4mm (1/8in) silk ribbon 3m (3 1/4yd) (20); 6m (6 5/8yd) (156); 3m (3 1/4yd) (13); 2m (2 1/4yd) (14)
- For daisies: YLI silk ribbon 6m x 4mm (6 5/8yd x 1/8in) (3); 3m x 4mm (3 1/4yd x 1/8in) (54); 4m x 2mm (4 3/8yd x 1/16in) (20); Anchor Stranded Cotton (844)
- For shrub flowers: YLI silk ribbon 4m x 2mm (4 3/8yd x 1/16in) (178); 4m x 2mm (4 3/8yd x 1/16in) (179); 3m x 4mm (3 1/4yd x 1/8in) (2); Anchor Stranded Cotton (263)
- For lavender: KNK 1,000 denier silk thread (827,192)
- For bow: 75cm x 32mm (30in x 1 1/2in) silk ribbon (178,158)
- No 18 chenille needle
- No 20 and No 22 chenille needles
- No 5 straw needle
- Fabric pencil

NOTE: see pattern sheet for placement of flowers

NOTE: this is an inspirational project. The diagram gives a guide to positioning the larger flowers. You may choose to follow this closely or change it to personal preference. By putting in the large flowers first, you can add as many or as few of the smaller blooms as you choose to create your own spring bouquet.

STITCHES USED

Ribbon Stitch, French Knot,

Stem Stitch, Bullion Stitch, Fly Stitch,

Folded Ribbon Roses

ing petal to give a shadow effect, taking care not to stitch through any of the petals and flatten the effect.

With the 7mm (¼in) ribbon (5), add three or four petals to form the rose bowl. Using Ribbon Stitch, pull the ribbon through until it curls, but then pull it back to loosen the petal and give a three dimensional look. You may need to add a couple of extra petals to achieve the required shape of the rose.

With a No 22 crewel needle, thread 4mm (⅛in) ribbon (158). Sew in some French Knots (two twists) to define the

centre of the rose. Draw in the stems, add the single buds in two or three Ribbon Stitches and leaves in clusters of three Ribbon Stitches.

CHRYSANTHEMUMS

Thread a No 20 chenille needle with 4mm (⅛in) ribbon (156). Starting from the centre and working outward, sew in petals using Ribbon Stitch. Complete a full circle.

Thread needle with 4mm (⅛in) ribbon (13) and work over the top of the first colour, coming out only half the

length of the petals. When you have completed the circle, sew five small petals in the centre using 4mm (⅛in) ribbon (14).

For the chrysanthemum buds, work four to five Ribbon Stitch petals. The stems are two strands of stranded cotton (844), worked in Stem Stitch. With 4mm (⅛in) ribbon (20) in the No 22 chenille, stitch fern-like leaves in Ribbon Stitch coming off the main stems.

DAISIES

Thread a No 22 chenille needle with 4mm (⅛in) ribbon (3). Draw a small circle for the centre. Using Ribbon Stitch, start from the centre of the daisy and work outward, making sure some petals cross over other petals, some are shorter than others, and there is a gap between some petals. This will make the daisy look more realistic.

With the same needle, thread 4mm (⅛in) ribbon (54). Fill the centre of the daisy with French Knots made with one twist of ribbon.

To create a shadow around the centre of the daisy, thread two strands of stranded cotton (844) and place a row of French Knots half way around the circle. Continue with two strands of cotton (844) and stitch in all the stems using Stem Stitch.

For the daisy buds, work Ribbon Stitch with a few French Knots at the base in stranded cotton. Thread a No 22 chenille needle with 2mm (¹⁄₁₆in) ribbon (20) and, working in Ribbon Stitch, create fern-like leaves coming off the main stems as shown in close-up.

SHRUB FLOWER SPRAY

Thread a No 22 chenille needle with 2mm (¹⁄₁₆in) ribbon (178). With Ribbon Stitch, sew six or seven petals around the top half of a circle. Add a few shadow petals in between with 2mm (¹⁄₁₆in) silk ribbon (179).

On the bottom half of the circle, add some green leaves with 4mm (⅛in) rib-

bon (21). Add a few purple petals over the green leaves.

Thread two strands of stranded cotton (263) and sew a Straight Stitch from each petal to the base of the flower. Stem Stitch the stem.

LAVENDER

Thread a No 5 straw needle with KNK silk thread (827). Starting at the top of the stem with Bullion Stitch, stitch two eight-wrap bullions side by side. Leaving a small gap under the first two bullions, add three bullions with nine wraps. Continue in this manner, adding an extra bullion and an extra wrap, until you reach five bullions. Continue down the stem repeating five bullions until you achieve the desired effect.

With KNK silk thread (192), sew a Fly Stitch around the first bullion; continue down the stem sewing a Fly Stitch around each flower head. Complete the lavender by adding the stem in Stem Stitch.

FINISHING

Stretch the embroidered cushion face by spraying the back of the fabric with water and stretching over a board. Secure all round with nails about 2.5cm (1in) apart. Leave to dry and the fabric will shrink taut. Carefully remove the fabric from the board. Line the face with calico or similar weight fabric. Overlock the edges.

The cushion photographed was made with two frills cut on the cross. For the wider contrast frill, cut bias strips 25cm (10in) wide to length desired for fullness. For the narrower frill, cut bias strips 20cm (8in) wide and the same length as previously. Join the matching strips. Fold in half lengthwise and press. Gather both frills together. Cover No 3 piping cord with main or contrast fabric. Cut cushion back (allowing for zipper) from remaining contrast fabric. Make up cushion in the usual manner.

Jonquils and Irises

*Spring bulbs depicted in fresh bright colours are stitched in silk ribbon
to make this delightful picture. Just two different flower styles
form the design, making it a perfect first project for those who wish
to try their hand at silk ribbon embroidery.*

PREPARATION

Press linen fabric and fit into working frame or hoop. Mark the area for stitching. Use the photograph on page 71 as a guide for ribbon colours and placement of the flowers, which are positioned roughly in three uneven rows.

IRISES

Iris blooms are worked in white, purple, burnt apricot, cobalt blue, bright yellow, hot pink and soft apricot. Using ribbon and a size 18 needle, work the top petal of the irises in a Lazy Daisy Stitch (See page 165). Stitches for the iris should have a soft tension. The bottom petals are worked as a single stitch by bringing the needle up at 1 and passing it between the Lazy Daisy Stitch and the fabric at 2, then entering the fabric at 3.

Make a couple of iris buds by working a single Straight Stitch.

Work iris stems by stitching either four or five Straight Stitches using either colour of Coton à Broder, and working with a size 24 chenille needle.

JONQUILS

Work the petals in Straight Stitches and bright yellow silk ribbon with a size 20 chenille needle. Straight Stitches for the jonquil should be pulled firmly. A full bloom has six petals, which are best worked by bringing the needle up at points around a circular area (at each consecutive number on Diagram C on page 70) and down into the fabric at the centre. Work some flowers with only 3, 4 or 5 petals to give the impression of a side view of the flower.

Stitch buds by working two or three straight stitches (Diagram D).

Work the jonquil centre by making a small French Knot (one twist) using two

FINISHED SIZE

- 24cm x 20cm (10in x 8in)

MATERIALS

- 35cm (14in) square of cream linen
- 4mm (⅛in) silk ribbon in the following colours: white, purple (84), burnt apricot (88), cobalt blue (118), hot pink (153), soft apricot (167), bright yellow (121)
- DMC Coton à Broder in pistachio green light (368) and hunter green (3346). If desired this thread can be substituted for three strands of six-stranded embroidery thread
- DMC Stranded Embroidery Cotton in tangerine (740)
- No 18 to 24 chenille needles
- Embroidery frame or hoop

STITCHES USED

Lazy Daisy Stitch, Straight Stitch, French Knot

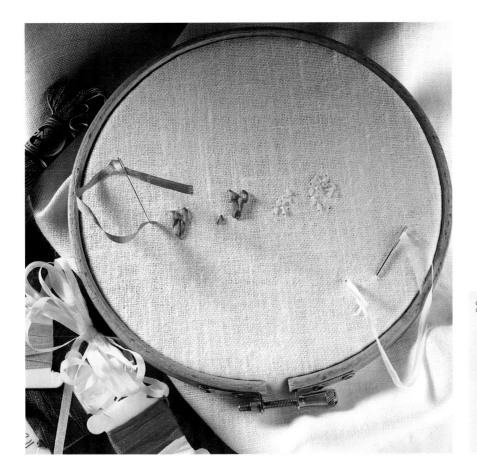

 HELPFUL HINT

When stitching, fabric should be held in an embroidery hoop or frame to avoid puckering. When working the iris flower, the tension of the stitch should be left quite loose, but the jonquil stitches need to be pulled firmly.

A

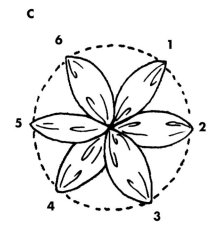

B

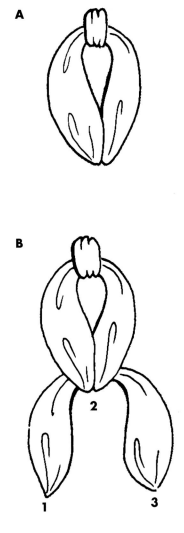

C

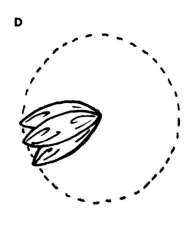

D

Iris

Jonquil

strands of tangerine (740) thread.

Stitch stems in single Straight Stitches as for irises.

Work your initials in one corner and press fabric carefully from the back, but do not press over embroidered area.

Your work is now ready for framing. Take it to a professional framer who is experienced in framing needlework. This way you will have a beautifully presented piece that will be an heirloom to treasure.

Detail of the embroidery shows colour and stitch placement. Flower stems have been worked with Coton à Broder thread in hunter green and light pistachio green.

Autumn Cushion

*A beautiful blending of ribbons and threads in rich
autumnal hues combine to make this sumptuous cushion
an irresistible temptation for any experienced
needleworker eager to hone their skills.*

PREPARATION

Cut a 43cm (17in) square piece of damask or your chosen fabric for the cushion face.

Overlock the edges to prevent fraying. Fold fabric in half, vertically and horizontally to find the centre. You may wish to run a line of basting stitches along the fold lines to mark the quarters and help in balancing the design. The basting will be removed after completing the embroidery.

You may prefer to draw the design onto a sheet of paper first. Otherwise, draw in the stems of the flower groups using a water-soluble pen. Work one group before drawing in the next. Alternatively, you may prefer to work completely freehand.

EMBROIDERY

ROSES

Make three handmade roses (refer to Diagram 1 on page 74) using the ribbons specified in the table on page 77. Make each rose in a different colour. With two strands of embroidery cotton to match the roses, attach to the centre of the cushion square.

LEAVES

With a No 18 chenille needle, thread a 35cm (14in) length of rayon ribbon and stitch the leaves around the roses using Ribbon Stitch. For some of the leaves use the sheer ribbon to give a shadow effect. Stitch the stems in Stem Stitch using a No 5 milliner's needle and two strands of olive green Anchor Stranded Cotton.

FINISHED SIZE

- 43cm (17in) square (including ruched edging)

MATERIALS

- 50cm (20in) square furnishing damask for cushion
- Fabric for cushion back
- Ribbons (see table p77)
- Threads (see table p77)
- Stranded cotton to match roses
- No 18 and 20 chenille needles
- No 1, 3 and 5 milliner's needles
- Long No 17 darner
- Mill Hill Glass Beads (03004)
- Water-soluble pen
- 1.5m (1⅝yd) braid (optional)
- 4 x tassels (optional)
- 2m (2¼yd) of your preferred edging (optional)

NOTE: this is an inspirational project and no diagram is given. Follow the photograph for the positioning of the roses and buds, then place the other flowers in relation to them. We have reproduced sections of the stitch work to make it easier to follow if you wish to follow this design closely. Alternatively, you may prefer to use the stitch placement as a guide only.

STITCHES USED

Folded Ribbon Roses, Ribbon Stitch,

Straight Stitch, French Knot, Bullion Stitch,

Lazy Daisy Stitch, Stem Stitch

Folded Ribbon Rose
Fold the ribbon until it reaches the fullness you want.

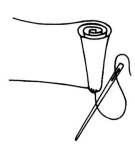

1. Fold raw edge down a little, then roll ribbon three or four times to form centre of rose. Secure with three or four stitches.

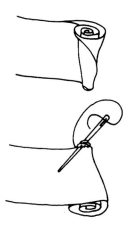

3. Pull centre of rose down so when you roll it into the ribbon it will be level with the top of the fold. Stitch the base of the rose after each fold.

2. Fold ribbon on the cross. Each fold of ribbon is a petal.

4. Keep folding and stitching until you have the size and shape you want. To finish, stitch the ribbon at the bottom of the rose to prevent fraying.

Diagram 1
Folded Ribbon Rose

ROSE BUDS

Make two buds to match each rose. Fold the ribbon around and cross it over in the front (keeping the sheer ribbon on the outside).

Gather the bottom of the bud and stitch to secure. Stitch in place around the roses.

Add two green ribbon stitches around the bottom of each bud. Stitch in some stems using two strands of cotton.

Each fold of ribbon becomes a petal, so you will not need many turns to complete a bud.

SPENT ROSE HEADS

With rayon ribbon and No 18 chenille needle, Straight Stitch five petals facing downwards. With two strands of olive green Anchor Stranded Cotton, add Straight Stitches from the top of the petals. With two strands of tan Marlitt thread in a No 5 milliner's needle, stitch a group of French Knots until the top of the head is nicely covered. Sew in the stems with two strands of olive green Anchor, curving the Stem Stitch slightly toward the roses.

BLOSSOM FLOWERS

Using a length of gold georgette ribbon in a No 18 chenille needle, stitch five petals in Ribbon Stitch. Stitch three French Knots at the centre using 4mm (1/8in) gold silk ribbon. Sew a cluster of Mill Hill glass beads around the French Knots until the centre is completely filled.

BUDS

With a length of gold georgette ribbon and a No 18 chenille needle, stitch two Ribbon Stitches side by side. Add Straight Stitches in 4mm (1/8in) green silk ribbon either side of the bud and one at the centre. The stem is couched in the same silk ribbon. Be sure not to pull the ribbon too tightly or it will lose its full effect.

FERN LEAVES

Thread a No 20 chenille needle with either 4mm (⅛in) leaf green or dark olive green silk ribbon. The fern is stitched in Ribbon Stitch, working alternately to the left and the right to form a vein. Continue stitching until you have a leaf shape (work in the same way as you would if using thread and Satin Stitch). Work stems in Stem Stitch using two strands of green cotton. Stitch some leaves in each of the green ribbons.

YUCCAS

Thread the No 17 darner with chenille. Work one 20 wrap Bullion Stitch for the yucca. Work three or four yuccas for each group. Add a Ribbon Stitch either side of the yucca head using 4mm (⅛in) grey/green silk ribbon. Work the stems in Stem Stitch using a No 5 milliner's needle and two strands of dark tan Anchor Stranded cotton.

BERRIES

Draw little circles on stems and fill in with French Knots using a No 1 milliner's needle and dark burgundy Nova thread. Over the top of these, add a few French Knots in dark wine Lola thread to give a nice rounded appearance.

Add a calyx in forest green Glory thread using a No 5 milliner's needle working a 10-wrap Bullion across the base of each berry. Continue to stitch the stem in Stem Stitch also using the forest green glory thread.

AUTUMN FORGET-ME-NOTS

Thread 4mm (⅛in) variegated silk ribbon in a No 20 chenille needle. For each flower, stitch five petals in Ribbon Stitch. Add a French Knot centre for each using 4mm (⅛in) gold silk ribbon. The sprays should taper off at the top with a few buds worked in a single Ribbon Stitch. Work stems by Stem Stitching in two strands of green Marlitt thread, then add the tiny Lazy Daisy leaves also in the green Marlitt.

BULLION SPRAYS

With the No 3 milliner's needle and two strands of tan Marlitt, stitch in the flower heads with 14-wrap Bullion Stitch. The top bud of each spray has three bullions, and the others have five, worked in a fan shape. Add the stems in Straight Stitches using two strands of the olive green Anchor cotton.

When the embroidery is complete, make up the cushion with a ruched edging (as shown), fringing or cord, whichever you prefer. You may also wish to add a braid around the edge of the cushion and tassels in each corner.

HELPFUL HINT

If the finished project will need occasional laundering, prewash the fabric to allow for shrinkage.

FLOWER	QUANTITY	RIBBON/THREAD
Roses and Buds	1.5m (1⅝yd) each	Mokuba 23mm (1in) poly/rayon 4599 ribbon in dark burgundy (15), rust (10) and dark purple (16)
	4.5m (4⅞yd)	Mokuba 25mm (1in) graduated 4881 ribbon in colour (4)
Leaves	2m (2¼yd)	Mokuba 25mm (1in) graduated rayon 4882 ribbon in colour (1)
	2m	Mokuba 25mm (1in) sheer organdy 1500 ribbon in green (18)
Stems	1 skein	Anchor Stranded Cotton olive green (845)
Spent Rose Heads	1.5m (1⅝yd)	Mokuba 12mm (⁷⁄₁₆in) graduated rayon ribbon in colour (1), Anchor Stranded Cotton olive green (845)
Blossom Flowers	2m (2¼yd)	Marlitt thread in tan (869). Mokuba 15mm crepe georgette 4546 in gold (14)
	1m (1⅛yd)	YLI 4mm (⅛in) silk ribbon in gold (54)
Fern Leaves	2m (2¼yd) each	YLI 4mm (⅛in) silk ribbon in leaf green (72) and dark olive green (171)
Yuccas	1pkt	Cotton on Creations chenille thread in copper/mauve comb
Leaves	2m (2¼yd)	YLI 4mm (⅛in) silk ribbon in blue/green (75)
Stems	1 skein	Anchor Stranded Cotton in dark tan (310)
Berries	1 skein each	Edmar Threads Nova dark burgundy (141), Lola dark wine (137)
Stems	1 skein	Edmar Threads Glory Forest green (110)
Autumn Forget-me-nots	5m (5½yd)	Hand-dyed silk ribbon 4mm (⅛in) variegated colour (6E)
	2m (2¼yd)	YLI 4mm (⅛in) silk ribbon in gold (54). Marlitt thread green (826)
Bullion Sprays		Marlitt thread tan (869)
Stems		Anchor Stranded Cotton olive green (845.

Bonnie the Bear Baby Blanket

What a wonderful gift for a new arrival!
This delightful bassinette blanket combines felt applique,
folded ribbon roses and wool and
silk ribbon embroidery.

PREPARATION

❖

Trace the outline of the bear and the barrow from the pattern sheet onto greaseproof paper. Cut the paper pattern for the bear 2cm (¾in) larger all round than the actual traced pattern. Pin the tracing in position on the blanket. (When placing your design, remember to allow for the turn back at the top and the tuck in at the bottom of the blanket. Bonnie's feet have been placed 34cm (13½in) from the bottom of the blanket).

Refer to pattern on pattern sheet. Transfer the bear outline to the blanket with tacking stitches worked through both the tracing and blanket. If you run the sharp end of the needle along the outline of the bear, the paper should be easy to tear and lift off, leaving you with the tacked outline and details of the bear.

When all the bear outlines have been tacked, remove the paper pattern.

Cut the paper pattern pieces the exact size of the barrow and wheels. Place on the appropriate felt and cut out. Pin the felt barrow in place. Use matching machine thread and small tacking stitches to secure the barrow and tack the wheels in place.

EMBROIDERY

❖

Using the beige tapestry wool, Stem Stitch around the tacked outline of the bear, removing the tacking thread as you work. Using two strands of brown stranded cotton, Satin Stitch the nose and the eye. Detail the eyelashes using Straight Stitch.

FINISHED SIZE

• 120cm x 70cm (48in x 32in)

MATERIALS

• Pure wool bassinette blanket

• 30cm x 6cm (12in x 2⅜in) felt for barrow

• 15cm x 6cm (6in x 2⅜in) felt for barrow wheels

• Machine thread to match felt

• Mokuba rayon ribbon: 75cm x 1cm (30in x ⅜in) wide of pink and cream

• Thread to match ribbons

• 3mm (⅛in) silk ribbon: 50cm (20in) very pale pink, 50cm (20in) pale blue, 1m (1⅛yd) pale pink

• 30cm x 1cm (12in x ⅜in) silk ribbon in colour of your choice for bow

• DMC Stranded Embroidery Cotton: one skein of brown (840)

• DMC Tapestry Wool: one skein each of pink (7200), peach (7853), lavender (7244), lemon (7745), blue (7800), green (7402), beige (7463), tan (7846), white (486) ·

• Appleton's Crewel Wool: one skein green (353)

• Greaseproof paper

• Size 18 chenille needle for wool embroidery and ribbon

• Size 8 crewel needle for stranded cotton

NOTE: see pattern sheet for design.

NOTE: wool felt is the most suitable for applique and is usually available from bear making suppliers.

STITCHES USED

Lazy Daisy Stitch, Straight Stitch, French Knot, Couching, Fly Stitch, Stem Stitch, Satin Stitch, Folded Ribbon Rose

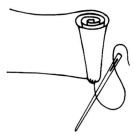

1. Fold raw edge down a little, then roll ribbon three or four times to form centre of rose. Secure with three or four stitches.

2. Fold ribbon on the cross. Each fold of ribbon is a petal.

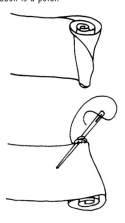

3. Pull centre of rose down so when you roll it into the ribbon it will be level with the top of the fold. Stitch the base of the rose after each fold.

4. Keep folding and stitching until you have the size and shape you want. To finish, stitch the ribbon at the bottom of the rose to prevent fraying.

Folded Ribbon Rose

FLOWERS IN THE BARROW

Work the ribbon roses next. Each rose requires about 20–25cm (8–10in) of ribbon. See Folded Ribbon Rose Diagram left. Stitch in place.

Using green tapestry wool, couch stems and work Lazy Daisy leaves.

For the daisies, work five Lazy Daisy petals with a French Knot centre. Use lemon, pink and peach tapestry wool for the petals with tan for the centres. Refer to photograph and design.

The forget-me-nots are five French Knots in blue tapestry wool, around a lemon French Knot centre. The lavender sprays are Straight Stitches worked in lavender tapestry wool. Refer to design.

Fill any remaining gaps between the flowers by adding French Knots in white tapestry wool and small leaves in green crewel wool.

Add the sprays of silk ribbon flowers. See photograph and design for placement. These are one, two or three Straight Stitches in very pale pink and pale blue, with a Fly Stitch in green crewel wool worked around each flower.

FIELD FLOWERS
UNDER THE BARROW

Work the stems in Straight Stitch using green tapestry wool. The flowers are two smaller Straight Stitches in pink, blue and white. Add a few French Knots in green at the base of the stems to fill any spaces.

Work a pale pink silk ribbon spray at the right hand side of the design, in the same manner as before. Add the daisy cluster and leaves at the top right hand of the design.

The finishing touch is the ribbon around Bonnie's neck. Take the 30cm (12in) length of your chosen silk ribbon. Bring the ends of the ribbon through on each side of the neck. A couple of stitches in machine cotton will secure the ribbon on the back of the work. Tie a bow and take the loose ends back through the work and secure. If you wish, you can catch down the tails of the bow in a couple of places with a French Knot.

See page 173 for information on laundering your blanket.

PLACEMENT GUIDE

KEY

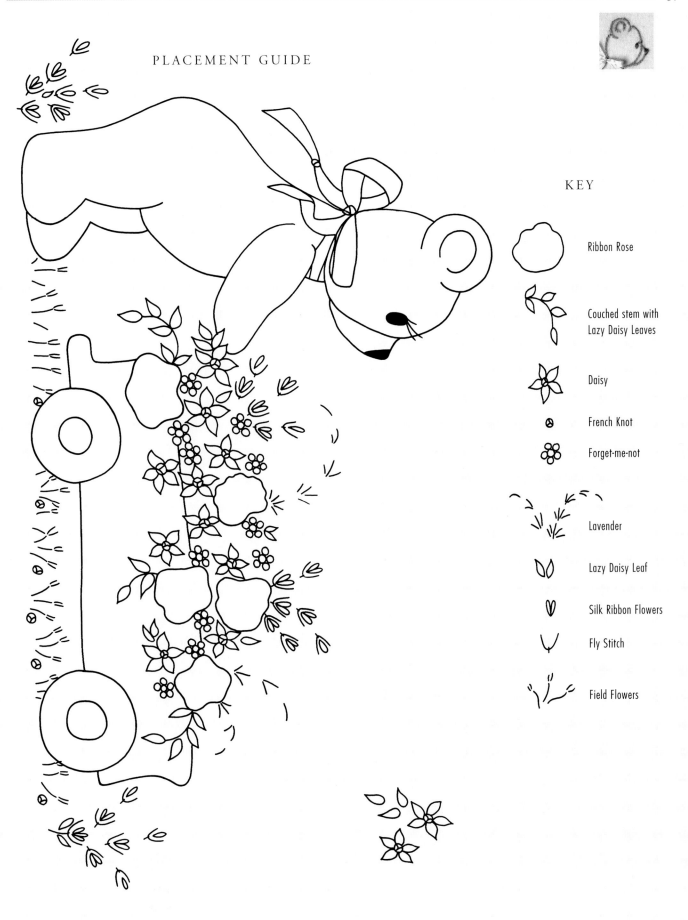

Ribbon Rose

Couched stem with
Lazy Daisy Leaves

Daisy

French Knot

Forget-me-not

Lavender

Lazy Daisy Leaf

Silk Ribbon Flowers

Fly Stitch

Field Flowers

Apple Blossom

*These silk-ribbon embroidered apple blossoms
flower all year round on a pretty porcelain bowl. Just two simple
ribbon embroidery stitches are required for the flowers, with details
added in stranded cotton — an ideal project for beginners.*

HELPFUL HINT

Beginners may find it helpful to practise the stitches and spreading the ribbon before starting work. To do this, keep the ribbon flat under the thumb on the surface and the first finger under the fabric. Bring the needle through the fabric, slide it under the ribbon and pull on the needle as you slide it back to the exit point. If the ribbon twists, it won't spread evenly.

PREPARATION

Use the No 18 chenille needle for ribbon embroidery and a fabric that will allow the needle to be pulled through easily. Work with only a 30cm (12in) length of ribbon and always cut the ribbon on an angle. Before you start to embroider, tie a firm knot in the end of the ribbon to secure your first stitch. Thread the ribbon

into the needle, but do not loop over the point of the needle as this tends to 'wear' the ribbon, particularly 7mm (¼in). To end off the ribbon, use a crewel needle and one strand of cotton. Sew the end of the ribbon to the back of the stitch.

An embroidery hoop or frame will allow you to maintain the correct tension. The sample was worked with a soft tension, allowing the width of the ribbon to remain full. A tighter tension reduces the size of the stitch.

EMBROIDERY

See the Stitch Guide on page 160 for stitch diagrams. Thread the white and pink ribbons together into the chenille needle. Embroider the apple blossom flower in Ribbon Stitch so the white ribbon lies on top of the pink. Add the centres in French Knots (two wraps),

FINISHED SIZE

- 7.5cm (3in) diameter

MATERIALS

- 7mm (¼in) YLI silk ribbon: 2m (2¼yd) white (3), 2m (2¼yd) pink (24), 1m (1⅛yd) dark green (75)
- 15cm (6in) square avocado green evenweave linen
- No 18 chenille needle (for ribbon)
- No 7 crewel needle (for stranded cotton)
- DMC Stranded Cotton: green (501), soft yellow (676)
- Framecraft medium round porcelain bowl with lid
- Embroidery hoop or frame

STITCHES USED

Ribbon Stitch, Straight Stitch,

Fly Stitch, French Knot

KEY

Straight Stitch

Ribbon Stitch

Ribbon
Stitch

Fly Stitch

 59%

This diagram has been enlarged for easier use.

using three strands of soft yellow cotton. The apple blossom buds are worked in one or two straight stitches. Complete the buds in Fly Stitch using three strands of green cotton. Work the stems in Straight Stitch, also using three strands of green cotton.

Work the leaves in Ribbon Stitch using dark green ribbon.

FITTING THE EMBROIDERED LID

❖

Remove the acetate and paper from the lid. Cut out your embroidered fabric and the supplied padding to the same size as the acetate.

Make a 'sandwich' of the embroi-
dered fabric (placed face down), the padding and the acetate. Place all three layers in the lid and secure with the metal locking disk following the instructions supplied with the bowl. Use strips of double sided tape to secure the lid liner to the metal disc.

Do not use glue as it may cause the liner to buckle when it has dried.

A Floral Abundance

Lavender and larkspur, apple blossoms and hollyhocks may sound like the backdrop to today's fashionable cottage garden but, in fact, as embroidered motifs these flowers have blossomed on textiles since the medieval era.

Miraculously, fragile examples still exist of 17th century crewelwork wall-hangings embroidered with foliage in sinuous patterns. Once they hung on the cold, stone walls of castles, affording a little warmth in the bitter chill of the English climate. The garden trend continued into the Elizabethan era, when not only were wall-hangings often embroidered with flowers and leaves, but furniture also underwent transformation. The passion for bright garish colours, as well as the geometric precision of the needlework patterns, burnt itself out. Soon the order of the day was for soft colours and harmonious patterns. The cottage garden fulfilled this need and became an inexhaustible source of inspiration for needleworkers and artists alike. We can be thankful that much of the early-20th century embroidered household linen has been preserved in pristine condition.

Wherever the embroidered flowers bloomed they brought with them their own symbol of romance, domestic tranquillity and friendship.

First Home Memories

The artist's picket fence and garden of her childhood home are remembered in this ribbon embroidery design. Set on a background colour-washed with FolkArt paints, the pretty springtime blooms and tiny spider's web evoke the halcyon days of childhood.

PREPARATION

Before starting work, prewash the fabric. If you omit this step and commence work, the fabric may shrink and pucker which will spoil the embroidery.

Cut a 40cm (15¾in) square of fabric for the cushion front. Place the design outline from the pattern sheet under the fabric and carefully mark in the fence pickets using a light touch and the Pygma pen. A light box or a sunlit window may be helpful here so that you can see the design through the fabric more easily. Allow the pen markings to dry completely before adding the colour wash to the fabric.

Using the water-soluble pen, draw a faint line to indicate the position of the painted background area as indicated by the dotted line on the design outline.

Place a small amount of paint onto a plate and using water to dilute, create a colour wash. Apply this inside the area marked with the dotted line. Apply only small amounts of colour wash at a time, building up gradually to the desired effect. If the fabric becomes too wet during the painting process, simply dry with a hair dryer to prevent the paint from bleeding into adjacent areas.

The concentrations of deeper colour should be kept in the foreground and the painted area allowed to fade out near the painted edge boundary. Refer to the photograph of the painted background design to determine where the colour wash is concentrated.

Allow the painted background to dry completely before commencing work.

Fit your fabric, with the design centred, into your hoop. The fabric should be drum tight. This tension is important for successful ribbon embroidery. It is best to remove the embroidery from the hoop when not working on it, to avoid making marks or permanent creases.

FINISHED SIZE

- 39cm (15½in) square (excluding frill)

MATERIALS

- 1m x 115cm (1⅛yd x 45in) cotton fabric (the sample was stitched on an all-over marbled design in cream and white)
- 1m x 115cm (1⅛yd x 45in) plain homespun fabric in sage green
- 2mm (1/16in) YLI silk ribbon: 50cm (20in) each of light blue green (32), medium blue green (33), medium sky blue (44); 1m (1⅛yd) each of white (3), medium glass green (20) and dark forest green (21)
- 4mm (⅛in) YLI silk ribbon: 50cm (20in) each of dark forest green (21), light ice green (62), light yellow green (170); 1m (1⅛yd) each of white (3), very pale pink (5), pale lemon (13), pale yellow (14), bright yellow (15), light mauve (22), light blue green (32), dark jungle green (72), purple (84), deep mauve (102), light blue (125); 3m (3¼yd) each of medium grass green (20) and very light rose pink (163)
- 7mm (¼in) YLI silk ribbon: 50cm (20in) medium grass green (20)
- 9mm (⅜in) Spark Organdy ribbon: 1m (1⅛yd) each of medium grass green (32) and light khaki (45)
- Rajmahal Art Silk thread: one skein each of laurel green (65), maidenhair (521), sassafras (805), verdigris (926), black (29)
- Kanagawa Silk Twist: one skein each of bright yellow (19), light grass green (160), deep dusky pink (821)
- Madeira Metallic Silver thread
- Fine crewel needles
- No 18 to 24 chenille needles
- Sharp embroidery scissors
- Blue water-soluble pen
- Brown .05 Pygma pen
- Plaid FolkArt paint in Clover (932) and Thicket (924)

(continued page 88)

✄ HELPFUL HINT

For Extended and Couched Ribbon Stitch (used at right), catch the ribbon using two small Straight Stitches across the width of the ribbon. Fold the ribbon over these stitches and complete the Ribbon Stitches. The Straight Ribbon Stitch leaves can be worked from top to bottom as well as from bottom to top for more economical use of the ribbon.

EMBROIDERY

The Kanagawa and Rajmahal threads are worked in a single strand throughout the entire design.

The numbers on the design outline indicate where the flowers are to be stitched. Refer to the chart on page 90 for stitches, thread/ribbon and colours for each group.

Following the design and the list of threads and ribbons used, complete each flower group. The water-soluble pen is useful here to allow you to draw in the stems and branches prior to working them. You may also find it useful to mark the centre only of the ground cover daisies, violets and forget-me-nots. Use the pen lightly and try to get into the habit of removing any marks with a wet cotton bud as soon as you finish each group. Some flower groups will need to be worked before others so that the front flowers can overlap in certain positions. Refer to photograph and positioning diagram to determine which flowers appear to be in front.

Begin by marking and stitching the stem of the wattle tree. The base of the tree is three rows of Stem Stitch worked closely together. Work the leaves randomly up the sides of each branch and add the flowers. Mark in and stitch the stem of the climbing rose. Work the Spider's Web Roses in the positions indicated. Add the rose buds and work a Fly Stitch around the bud and a Straight Stitch in the centre. Add the leaves in groups of three, five or as a single leaf.

The bluebells, snowdrops, lily of the valley, lavender, grape hyacinths and daisy bush can be worked at this stage. Refer to the chart. The pink flowering foliage and the two groups of violets can be added next. The violet flowers are formed with five Ribbon Stitches (two upper and three lower). Make the lower stitches slightly longer than the upper

stitches. Finally, add the detail stitching to the violet buds in the same way as the rose buds.

The lemon and pink ground cover daisies and their leaves are worked next. The pink daisies have five petals, the lemon daisies have seven. The leaves are worked in groups of two or three.

Next, work the two groups of forget-me-nots.

Work the spider's web among the flowers of your garden and add the spider. The web is worked in Straight Stitch using one strand of silver Madeira Metallic and the spider is a single-wrap French Knot in one strand of black Rajmahal thread.

Complete the embroidery by working your initials and the date in an unobtrusive position.

After completing the embroidery, remove the fabric from the hoop. Press the fabric around the embroidery with a steam iron to remove all the ridges left by the hoop. Don't iron ribbon embroidery.

MAKING UP

❖

Using a saucer or something similar as a template, round off the corners of the cushion front.

Cut three strips of fabric 20cm wide x 115cm (8in x 45in) from the front panel fabric. These strips form the inner frill. Join the strips together in a circle and press in half with the wrong sides together.

Cut three strips of fabric 24cm wide x 115cm (9¹/₂in x 45in) from the backing fabric to form the outer frill. Join and press as before. Check that the two circles of fabric are the same length. Fold the frills in half and press along the fold. Place the raw edges of both frills together and machine sew two rows of gathering

stitch along the raw edges – the first row 6mm (¼in) from the edge and the second row 10mm (⅜in) from the edge. Divide and mark your frills into quarters. Pin the frill evenly into position on the cushion front, one quarter of the frill to each side. Pull up the gathering threads and arrange the gathers evenly before sewing into position.

Back the cushion in your preferred method. Press the edges of the cushion avoiding the embroidery and place the cushion insert inside your cushion cover.

LAUNDERING

The FolkArt paints and Pygma pen are permanent once dry. Prewash the fabric before starting work to allow for any possible shrinkage. The cushion may be gently hand washed, using pure soap. Rinse well, dry in the shade. When ironing take care to avoid the embroidery. Lightly spraying water on the silk ribbon will encourage it to sit up as if it has just been completed.

FLOWER	THREAD/RIBBON/COLOUR	STITCH
1: Forget-me-nots		
Flower centre	Kanagawa (19)	1-wrap French Knot
Petals	4mm (1/8in) ribbon (125)	1-wrap French Knot
Leaves	4mm (1/8in) ribbon (62)	Ribbon Stitch
2: Violets		
Flower centre	Kanagawa (19)	1-wrap French Knot
Petals	4mm (1/8in) ribbon (84)	Ribbon Stitch
Buds	4mm (1/8in) ribbon (84)	Ribbon Stitch
Leaves	7mm (1/4in) ribbon (20)	Ribbon Stitch
Detail stitching	Rajmahal (521)	Fly and Straight Stitch
3: Bluebells		
Stems	Rajmahal (65)	Stem Stitch
Leaves	2mm (1/16in) ribbon (21)	Extended & Couched Ribbon St
Flowers	2mm (1/16in) ribbon (44)	Ribbon Stitch
Flower details	2mm (1/16in) ribbon (21)	Ribbon Stitch
4: Lemon Ground Cover Daisy		
Flower centre	Kanagawa (19)	1-wrap French Knot
Petals	4mm (1/8in) ribbon (13)	Ribbon Stitch
Leaves	4mm (1/8in) ribbon (21)	Ribbon Stitch
5: Wattle Tree		
Stem and branches	Kanagawa (160)	Stem Stitch
Leaves	4mm (1/8in) ribbon (20)	Ribbon Stitch
	9mm (3/8in) Spark Organdy (32)	Ribbon Stitch
	9mm (3/8in) Spark Organdy (45)	Ribbon Stitch
Flowers	4mm (1/8in) ribbon (14)	1-wrap French Knot
	4mm (1/8in) ribbon (15)	1-wrap French Knot
6: Snowdrops		
Leaves	2mm (1/16in) ribbon (20)	Extended Ribbon Stitch
Flowers	2mm (1/16in) ribbon (3)	Ribbon Stitch
Stems	Rajmahal (521)	Straight Stitch
Flower details	Rajmahal (521)	French Knot
7: Pale Pink Ground Cover Daisies		
Flower centre	Kanagawa (821)	French Knot
Petals	4mm (1/8in) ribbon (5)	Ribbon Stitch
Leaves	4mm (1/8in) ribbon (32)	Ribbon Stitch
8: Lavender		
Stems	Rajmahal (805)	Stem Stitch
Flowers	4mm (1/8in) ribbon (22)	1-wrap French Knot
Leaves	2mm (1/16in) ribbon (33)	Ribbon Stitch

FLOWER	THREAD/RIBBON/COLOUR	STITCH
9: Lily of the Valley		
Leaves	2mm (1/16in) ribbon (21)	Extended Ribbon Stitch
Stems	Rajmahal (65)	Stem Stitch
Flowers	2mm (1/16in) ribbon (3)	1-wrap French Knot
10: Climbing Rose		
Stem	Rajmahal (521)	Stem Stitch
Flowers	4mm (1/8in) ribbon (163)	Spider's Web Rose
Flower buds	4mm (1/8in) ribbon (163)	Ribbon Stitch
Bud details	Rajmahal (521)	Fly & Straight Stitch
Leaves	4mm (1/8in) ribbon (72)	Ribbon Stitch
11: Grape Hyacinths		
Leaves	4mm (1/8in) ribbon (170)	Ribbon Stitch
Stems	Rajmahal (521)	Stem Stitch
Flowers	4mm (1/8in) ribbon (102)	1-wrap French Knot
12: Lemon Ground Cover Daisies		
Work as for No 7		
13: Pink Flowering Foliage		
Stems	Rajmahal (926)	Stem Stitch
Leaves	2mm (1/16in) ribbon (32)	Ribbon Stitch
Flowers	4mm (1/8in) ribbon (5)	1-wrap French Knot
14: White Daisy Bush		
Leaves	4mm (1/8in) ribbon (20)	Extended & Couched Ribbon Stitch
Petals	4mm (1/8in) ribbon (3)	Ribbon Stitch
Flower centres	Kanagawa (19)	1-wrap French Knot
Flower buds	4mm (1/8in) ribbon (3)	Ribbon Stitch
Flower details	Rajmahal (521)	Fly & Straight Stitch
Stems	Rajmahal (521)	Straight Stitch
15: Forget-me-nots		
Work as for No 1.		
16: Violets		
Work as for No 2.		
17: Pale Pink Ground Cover Daisies		
Work as for No 7.		

Poppies in the Wild

*This striking picture of vibrant red poppies is fresh
and appealing. The construction of the flowers and
the stitching of the stems and grasses are simple,
yet wonderfully effective and eye catching.*

PREPARATION

If you have already purchased your frame, draw around the opening with a 3B pencil on the back of the fabric. This provides perimeters for your work and serves as a stitching guide. The design is worked from the base of the outline, to within 12mm (½in) of the top.

If you are not using a purchased frame, mark the working area, 9cm (3½in) high by whatever width you choose, on the back of the fabric.

It is recommended that you use a hoop to keep your tension even on long stitches. You may need to add some calico to the sides of the linen to fit in a frame large enough to expose the entire working area.

EMBROIDERY

The poppies are worked first, then the 'greenery' is worked around them. To make a poppy, cut three strips of 13mm (½in) ribbon approximately 7cm (3in) long. Lay them one over another forming a star, with the curl of the ribbon (if it is apparent) facing up. Knot the bottom of two strands of Madeira green stranded silk several times in the same spot to create a 'lump' on the end of the thread. Cut the tail off very close to the knot and take the thread through the three pieces of poppy ribbon from front to back. Fold the ribbon in half (so the knot is enclosed in the middle).

Still using the two strands of Madeira green silk, attach the poppy to the linen securely with a few Whip Stitches, then work a stem in Stem Stitch. The flowers should hover randomly 12mm (½in) or more from the top line and the bottom of the stems and grasses should finish at the lower line.

To 'cup' the poppy so that it stands up, take a long piece of polyester sewing thread and fold it into four. Make a loop and place it over the poppy so that it sits on the linen. Pull it up firmly and wrap it around and around the base of the flower to raise it up a little. Thread the ends into a needle and take them through to the back of the work and neaten off.

Using two strands of black Madeira stranded silk, work the centre of the poppy in Satin Stitch over the knot in the middle of the flower, cover it completely working over it several times to create a raised centre. Using one strand of rich gold Madeira Decora, work French Knots around the outside of the raised black centre. Use a fine No 9 crewel needle and take care when piercing the ribbon as it is very fragile.

With the Kacoonda pale green ribbon, work long Ribbon Stitches, varying the angle of these 'stems' so that they spread in various directions. Begin at the baseline of the work area and extend towards the top line. Do not return to the baseline to begin the next stitch. Carry the ribbon across the top line and work from top to bottom. Alternate this so that the minimum amount of ribbon is wasted and unnecessary bulk is avoided at the back of the work. Add more stems and grasses in Straight Stitch using pale lime green ribbon and Pistil Stitch using the brown silk ribbon. Position these stitches behind and in front of the previously worked stitches.

Using the silk twist, work long Straight Stitches and some Pistil Stitches over the top, through and underneath the ribbon stems. Vary the length and angle they are worked in.

Using three or four strands of the Waterlilies thread, fill the lower line with short Straight Stitches and Lazy Daisy Stitches. Finally, trim the corners of the poppy petals to give a rounded shape. Don't forget to sign and date your work. Frame as desired.

DESIGN AREA

- 27cm x 10cm (10½in x 4in)

MATERIALS

- 25cm (10in) handkerchief linen
- Kacoonda hand-dyed silk ribbon: 1m x 7mm (1⅛yd x ¼in) pale green
- YLI silk ribbon: 1.5m x 13mm (1⅝yd x ½in) poppy red (2); 1.5 x 4mm (1⅝yd x ¼in) each of brown (165), pale lime green (170)
- Kanagawa 1000 denier silk twist: pale green (161) and olive green (827)
- Madeira stranded silk: medium green (1311) and black
- Madeira Decora: rich gold (1571)
- Waterlilies by Caron silk thread: antique brass
- Polyester sewing thread to match the poppy ribbon
- No 18 to 24 chenille needles
- No 9 crewel needle
- Purchased frame with opening 27cm x 10cm (10½in x 4in) (optional)
- Embroidery hoop larger than the size of your embroidery
- 3B pencil

STITCHES USED

Fly Stitch, Stem Stitch, Satin Stitch, Ribbon Stitch, Straight Stitch, Lazy Daisy Stitch, French Knot, Pistil Stitch

Floral Fantasy

The completed work of delicate ribbon flowers
worked in satin-edged crepe georgette,
wire-edged organza and silk ribbons is shown to perfection
in a custom-made display box designed to sit on a tabletop.

PREPARATION

Place the square of silk over the design given on page 98 and transfer the markings with 2B pencil. For ribbon flowers, mark only the bases and centres. Mark the stamens. Do not transfer the numbers marked on the design.

Place the traced silk over the ecology cloth, centring the two layers. Tack together around the edges and through the centre (see broken line on design) using ecru machine thread.

Stitch the fabric layers to the tapestry frame according to the frame instructions. Tighten so fabric is held taut.

RIBBON FLOWERS

Refer to design and stitch key on page 98. Work in numerical order.

LARGE ORGANZA FLOWER

Cut 20cm (8in) length of wire-edged ecru ribbon. Using machine thread, run a gathering thread lengthwise down the centre of the ribbon. Gather up tightly and end off firmly. Stitch the flower to the design, tucking in the raw edges of the ribbon. Use machine thread and a fine straw needle. Stitch through the middle of the flower until you achieve the shape you are after.

MULBERRY FLOWER

Cut 12cm (4¾in) of mulberry ribbon. Gather up as for organza flower. Stitch into place and tuck in the raw edges as before. Secure to fabric with fine straw needle and machine thread, making sure the stitching is not visible.

PINK SILK FLOWERS

Cut a 15cm (6in) length of silk ribbon. Cut each end at a 45-degree angle as shown in Diagram 1. Work a gathering stitch along the shortest edge. Gather up

and end off firmly. Hold points A and B, and stitch these to the background fabric. Tease out the ruffled edge of the flower and stitch through the centre of the flower so that it is firmly held in place. Cut off any visible ends of ribbon. Thread a needle with three strands DMC light old gold (676) and work five two-wrap French Knots in the centre of each flower.

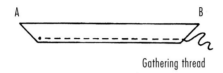

Diagram 1

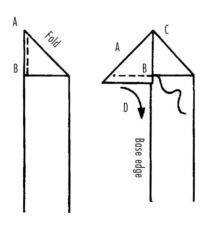

Diagram 2   *Diagram 3*

LARGE ECRU BUDS

Cut a 20cm (8in) length of ecru crepe georgette ribbon.

Fold one corner forward on the diagonal as shown in Diagram 2. Work a running stitch from A to B with machine thread. Now fold the ribbon to the back at C as shown in Diagram 3. Gather up the first stitching and begin to roll the ribbon from the end marked A. Keep rolling in the direction of the arrow D. Now fold the ribbon forward on the diagonal and roll. Do this three times, stitching through the base edge to keep all the folds in place.

DESIGN AREA

- 27cm x 25cm (10½in x 10in)

MATERIALS

- 45cm (17¾in) square dupion or Thai silk
- 50cm (19½in) square ecology cloth
- 25mm (1in) Mokuba crepe georgette ribbon: 1.8m (2yd) ecru, 1.6m (1¾yd) pink, 1m (1⅛yd) mulberry
- 38mm (1½in) wire-edged organza ribbon: 80cm (⅞yd) ecru
- 7mm (¼in) YLI silk ribbon: 1.2m (1⅜yd) pink
- DMC Stranded Embroidery Cotton: one skein each of medium khaki green (3012), fern green (522), light old gold (676), medium antique mauve (316), light antique violet (3042),
- 1.75m x 5cm (2yd x 2in) ecru Swiss embroidery or similar lace edging (optional)
- No 3 and 9 straw needles
- 60cm (24in) tapestry frame
- Ecru cotton machine thread
- 2B pencil

STITCHES USED

French Knot, Split Back Stitch, Satin Stitch, Pistil Stitch, Cretan Stitch, Straight Stitch, Buttonhole Stitch

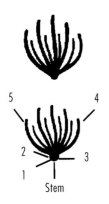

5   4

2   3

1

Stem

Diagram 4

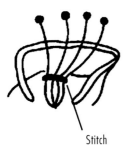

Stitch

Diagram 5

Form one last fold to end off the ribbon. Stitch cut ribbon end securely. Trim off any stray ends. Stitch the base of the bud to the silk design. Trim again. End off thread.

LARGE PINK BUDS

Cut 20cm (8in) lengths of pink georgette ribbon. Work as large ecru buds, making sure the tension is not too tight.

SMALL ECRU BUDS

Cut 12cm (4¾in) lengths of ecru georgette ribbon. Work as large buds but make only one fold, plus one fold to end off.

MULBERRY BUDS

Cut 12cm (4¾in) lengths of mulberry ribbon, work as for small ecru buds.

When all the ribbon flowers and buds are attached, it is time to add the thread embroidered details.

EMBROIDERY

Bud Base

Thread a straw needle with two strands medium khaki green (3012) together with two strands fern green (522). Work Satin Stitches as shown in Diagram 4. The stitching should cover the base of the bud. Make the stitches of varying lengths, but use the same base hole. When you are satisfied with the base of the bud, work one Straight Stitch for the stem of the mulberry buds, or Split Back Stitch for the longer stems of the ecru buds. Work five more Straight Stitches as indicated in Diagram 4.

Stamens

Thread a needle with three strands of light old gold (676) for the pink buds and large ecru buds. Use two strands of medium khaki green (3012) together with two strands of fern green (522) for the small ecru buds. The stamens of the mulberry buds are worked in two strands of fern green (522) and two strands of light old gold (676).

Work Pistil Stitch for all stamens. Come up inside the tube area of each bud, so this will not be seen when viewed from above. Work the number of stamens given in the design. Work a small stitch over the stamens as shown in Diagram 5, pulling them together and making them more secure.

Stems

Using two strands medium khaki green (3012) plus two strands fern green (522), work a Split Back Stitch along all of the stems.

Leaves

Using four strands of cotton as for stems, work Cretan Stitch using eight stitches. Commence at A on Diagram 6 and work down the leaf following outline and marked centre as a stitch guide.

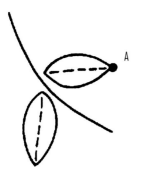

For the flower centres, work a single-wrap French knot using three strands of light old gold (676).

With your finger, gently push up the second row of Buttonhole Stitching to give the flower a cupped appearance.

Diagram 6

MAKING UP

❖

Buttonhole Stitch Flowers

Thread a needle with one strand each of medium antique mauve (316) and light antique violet (3042). Work Buttonhole Stitch around the outer circle, stitching into the centre hole. Finish off by stitching into the loop of the first Buttonhole Stitch. Now work Buttonhole Stitch around the outer edge, stitching into the previously worked Buttonhole Stitch loops. Use the eye of the needle to push through each loop. End off by passing the thread through the first stitch. Take the thread to the back of the work, close to the edge of the finished stitching. The smallest circle should be worked without the second row of Buttonhole Stitch.

Remove the work from the embroidery frame. Press around the embroidered area. Remove the tacking stitches being careful to avoid the stitching.

The piece is now ready to be framed or put into a display box as pictured. The piece was stretched over a 38cm (15in) square of plywood, padded with a layer of batting. The box was specially made to fit the finished piece. After being stretched over the plywood and laced with extra-strong thread, the wide ecru Swiss embroidery was cut into four lengths, the corners mitred and seam allowances trimmed back to 1cm (⅜in). Position the edging over the silk and stitch to the silk around the outer edge. A few stitches in each mitred corner will hold the edge in place.

KEY

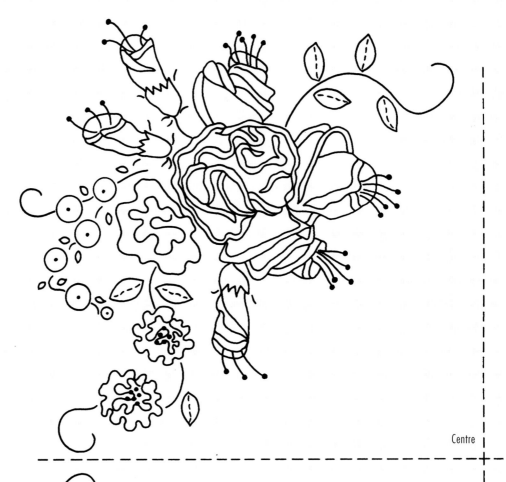

To align design, place the central
dotted lines on top of each other

Centre

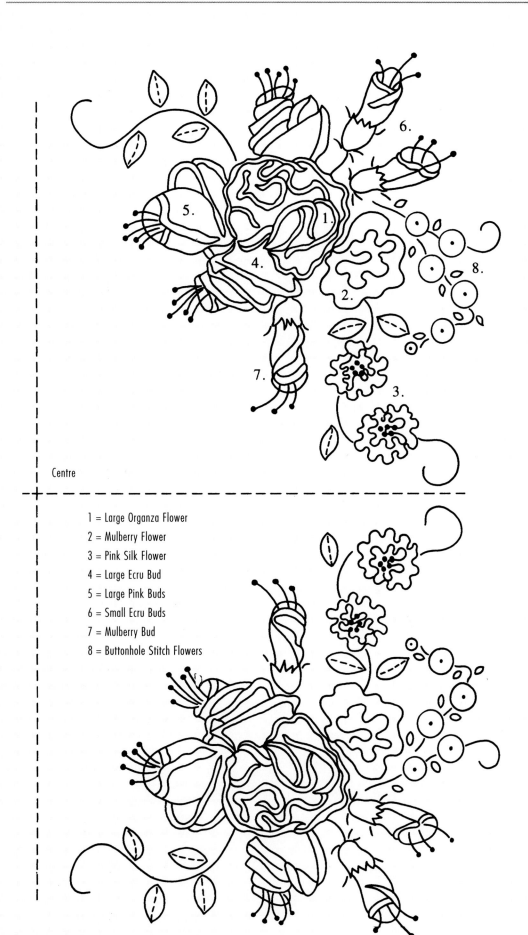

Centre

1 = Large Organza Flower
2 = Mulberry Flower
3 = Pink Silk Flower
4 = Large Ecru Bud
5 = Large Pink Buds
6 = Small Ecru Buds
7 = Mulberry Bud
8 = Buttonhole Stitch Flowers

104%

Spring Garden Ribbon Embroidery

*Anemones, liliums and freesias capture
the beauty of a spring garden landscape with this
simple colourwash using folk art paint
to add depth to the embroidery.*

PREPARATION

Centre the lid of the box on your fabric and use the water-soluble pen to draw a line around the cut-out. This line will form the external boundary of your embroidery work.

Also use the lid of the box to accurately cut a piece of thin batting which will be used to pad the embroidery. Using the placement diagram on page 105 and water-soluble pen, draw in the major stems and flower positions. This will give you a good indication where to apply the colourwash.

PAINTING BACKGROUND

Mix a very small amount of Plaid Clover (923) paint with a little water to create a watercolour consistency wash. Using a bristle brush, dab the wash onto the fabric gradually building up the depth of the colour in the foreground and decreasing the depth of colour near the edges of the embroidery. Allow this to dry completely.

Once again, using the positioning diagram, mark in the stems of the major flower groups with the water-soluble marking pen.

EMBROIDERY

Use No 18 chenille needle for 4mm (⅛in) and 7mm (¼in) ribbon, No 20 or 22 chenille needle for 2mm (¹⁄₁₆in) ribbon and the No 9 crewel needle for thread embroidery.

Fit your fabric into the hoop. The 30cm (12in) hoop will allow you to complete the embroidery without removing

DESIGN AREA

- 23cm x 17cm (9in x 6½in)

MATERIALS

- 40cm (16in) square seeded homespun fabric

- Lidded box with cut-out

- 2mm (1¹⁄₁₆in) YLI silk ribbons: 1.5m (1⅝yd) pale lemon (13), 1m (1⅛yd) very pale pink (5),1m (1⅛yd) pale pink (8), 1m (1⅛yd) deep mauve (23),1m (1⅛yd) raspberry pink (128) 0.5m (½yd) medium grape (179), 0.5m (½yd) light caramel (65), 0.5m (½yd) dark forest green (21), 1m (⅛yd) light blue green (32)

- 4mm (⅛in) YLI silk ribbons: 0.25m (¼yd) dark jungle green (72), 1m (1⅛yd) pale lemon (13), 1.5m (1⅝yd) medium grass green (20), 1m (1⅛yd) white (3), 0.5m (½yd) very light rose pink (163), 0.25m (¼yd) dark forest green (21), 2m (2¼yd) deep mauve (102) , 0.5m (½yd) bright yellow (15)

- 7mm (¼in) YLI silk ribbons: 0.5m (½yd) white (3), 0.5m (½yd) medium grass green (20)

- Rajmahal Art Silk: one skein each of maidenhair (521), Moroccan gold (94), grape (243), ecru, baby camel (45), laurel green (65), sassafras (805), black (29)

- Madeira machine thread in silver

- 30cm (12in) square thin batting

- 30cm (12in) embroidery hoop

- No 18 to 22 chenille needles

- No 9 crewel needle

- Water-soluble marking pen

- Plaid FolkArt acrylic paint in Clover (923)

- Bristle brush

- Paint requirements to finish box as desired

STITCHES USED

Stem Stitch,

Extended and Couched Ribbon Stitch,

Ribbon Stitch, French Knot,

Straight Stitch, Fly Stitch, Loop Stitch

Anther:
Straight Stitch

Stamen:
Stem Stitch

Petal Detail:
French Knots

Petals:
Ribbon Stitch

Stem:
Stem Stitch

Leaves:
Ribbon Stitch

Freesia

For Extended and Couched Ribbon Stitch (used at right), catch the ribbon using two small Straight Stitches across the width of the ribbon. Fold the ribbon over these stitches and complete the Ribbon Stitches. The Straight Ribbon Stitch leaves can be worked from top to bottom as well as from bottom to top for more economical use of the ribbon.

the fabric from the frame and without bruising any completed flowers.

The chart on page 104 gives the threads, ribbons and stitches used to create the individual flowers. The numbers refer to the position on the placement diagram. Separate diagrams are given for two new flower designs – freesias and liliums. You may choose to remove any pen marks either as you go or when the embroidery is complete. Gently dab marks with a cotton bud dipped in cold water. If marks are difficult to remove, cover the area with embroidery.

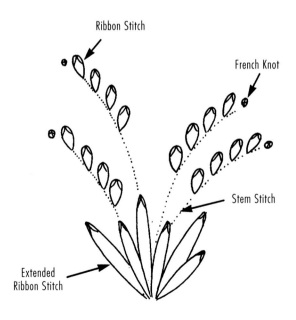

Ribbon Stitch

French Knot

Stem Stitch

Extended
Ribbon Stitch

Lilium

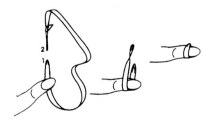

Looped Straight Stitch

PAINTING THE BOX

Give the entire box, inside and out, two coats of acrylic basecoat. The box photographed is a deep burgundy colour. Allow each coat to dry completely, then apply crackle medium to the external surfaces of the box. Allow to dry according to instructions given with the product.

Apply a cream top coat to the surfaces painted with crackle medium. Allow to dry well. An aged appearance can be created by rubbing the surface with a small amount of Burnt Umber acrylic on a soft cloth. Allow to dry, then apply a top coat of satin-finish clear acrylic varnish to protect all surfaces. If you'd like to frame your piece, take it to a professional framer.

FLOWER	THREAD/RIBBON	COLOUR	STITCH
1: Hyacinth			
Stem	Rajmahal (521)	Maidenhair	Stem Stitch
Leaves	4mm (1/8in) ribbon (72)	Dark jungle green	Extended Ribbon Stitch
Flowers	4mm (1/8in) ribbon (13)	Pale lemon	Single-wrap French Knot
2: Arum Lilies			
Stems	Rajmahal (521)	Maidenhair	Stem Stitch
Leaves	7mm (1/4in) ribbon (20)	Medium grass green	Ribbon Stitch
Flowers	7mm (1/4in) ribbon (3)	White	Ribbon Stitch
Flower detail	Rajmahal (94)	Moroccan gold	Straight Stitch
3: Liliums (see diagram page 102)			
Stems	Rajmahal (521)	Maidenhair	Stem Stitch
Leaves	4mm (1/8in) ribbon (20)	Medium grass green	Ribbon Stitch
Petals	4mm (1/8in) ribbon (3)	White	Ribbon Stitch
	4mm ribbon (1/8in) (163)	Very light rose pink	Ribbon Stitch
Petal details	Rajmahal (243)	Grape	French Knot
Stamens	Rajmahal ecru	Cream	Stem Stitch
Anthers	Rajmahal (45)	Baby camel	Straight Stitch
Flower Buds	4mm (1/8in) ribbon (3)	White	Ribbon Stitch
	4mm (1/8in) ribbon (163)	Very lightt rose pk	Ribbon Stitch
Bud details	Rajmahal (521)	Maidenhair	Fly/Straight Stitch
4: Grape Hyacinths			
Stems	Rajmahal (65)	Laurel green	Stem Stitch
Leaves	4mm (1/8in) ribbon (21)	Dark forest green	Extended and Couched Ribbon Stitch
Flowers	4mm (1/8in) ribbon (102)	Deep mauve	Single-wrap French Knot
5: Daffodils			
Leaves	2mm (1/16in) ribbon (32)	Light blue green	Extended and Couched Ribbon Stitch
Flower			
Trumpet	4mm (1/8in) ribbon (15)	Bright yellow	Loop Stitch
Petals	2mm (1/16in) ribbon (13)	Pale lemon	Ribbon Stitch
Buds	4mm (1/8in) ribbon (15)	Bright yellow	Ribbon Stitch
Stem/Bud details	Rajmahal (805)	Sassafras	Straight/Fly Stitch
6: Lily of the Valley			
Leaves	2mm (1/16in) ribbon (21)	Dark forest green	Extended and Couched Ribbon Stitch
Stems	Rajmahal (65)	Laurel green	Stem Stitch
Flowers	4mm (1/8in) ribbon (3)	White	Single-wrap French Knot
7: Anemones			
Stems	Rajmahal (521)	Maidenhair	Stem Stitch
Leaves	4mm (1/8in) ribbon (20)	Medium grass green	Ribbon Stitch
Flower petals	2mm (1/16in) ribbons (13), (5),(8), (23)	Pale lemon, very pale pink, pink, deep mauve	Ribbon Stitch
Flower	Rajmahal (29)	Black	Double-wrap centres French Knot
8: Freesias (see diagram page 102)			
Leaves	4mm (1/8in) ribbon (20)	Med grass green	Extended Ribbon Stitch
Stems	Rajmahal (521)	Maidenhair	Stem Stitch
Flowers	2mm (1/16in) ribbon (13)	Pale lemon	Ribbon Stitch/French Knot
9: Scattered Anemones			
Flower petals	2mm (1/16) ribbon (13), (5), (8), (128), (179), (65)	Pale lemon, very pale pink, pale pink, raspberry pink, medium grape, light caramel	Ribbon Stitch
Centres	Rajmahal (29)	Black	Double-wrap French Knot
Spider Web and Spider			
Web	Madeira machine thread	Silver	Straight Stitch
Spider	Rajmahal (29)	Black	Dble-wrap French Knot

DESIGN OUTLINE
AND
PLACEMENT DIAGRAM

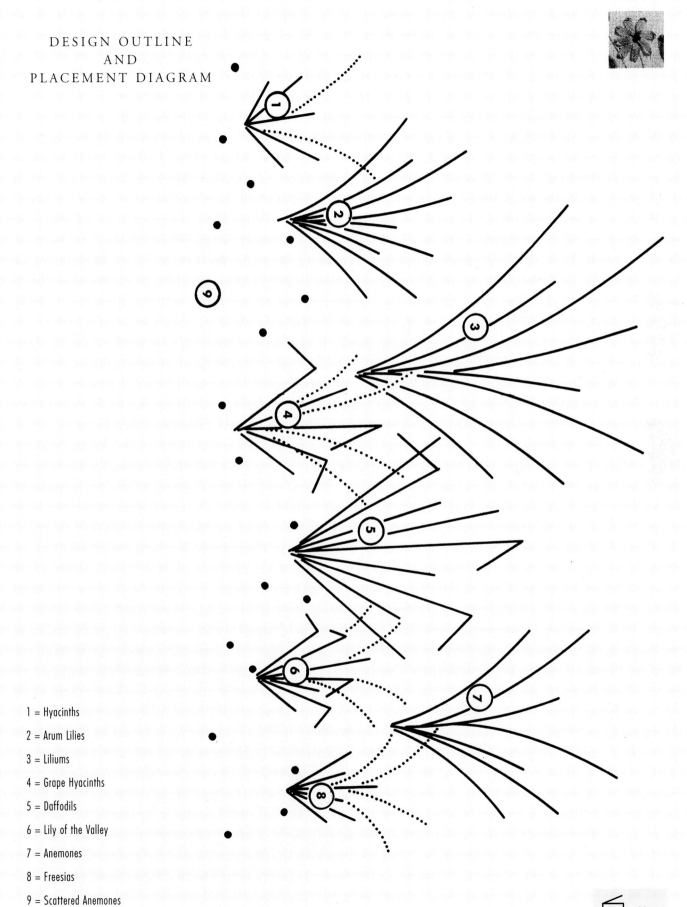

1 = Hyacinths

2 = Arum Lilies

3 = Liliums

4 = Grape Hyacinths

5 = Daffodils

6 = Lily of the Valley

7 = Anemones

8 = Freesias

9 = Scattered Anemones

SS

Basket of Flowers

An 18th century Sévres porcelain design was the inspiration
for this charming ribbon embroidered basket of flowers.
The linen background gives a wonderful matte contrast
to the soft lustre of the silk and satin ribbons.

PREPARATION

Trace the bare essentials of the design from page 109 onto tracing paper and transfer to the fabric with dressmaker's carbon paper. Only trace the lines of the garland, the bow and the basket. It is not difficult to work the flowers freehand from the design.

EMBROIDERY

Start with the basket, making 15 Straight Stitches in fawn satin ribbon for the ribs of the basket. Catch these stitches down along the edges with tiny stitches in one strand of matching cotton.

At the base of the basket, bring a length of fawn satin ribbon out at one side and twist it fairly tightly, stitching it down between each twist. Work two rows in this way, then a row of flat ribbon, then another two rows of twisted. Secure the flat ribbon by catching it along each side or working Herringbone Stitch in fawn stranded cotton.

For the top edge of the basket, work one row of twisted ribbon, then one row of flat and finally another row of twisted ribbon. Next, work the ribbon hanger

which comes right down to the basket (the flowers are worked over the ribbon). Cut the green satin ribbon in half. Tie one piece through the twisted ribbon at the side of the basket, leaving a short tail as shown on the pattern. Catch the tail in place here and there with one strand of matching thread. Do the same with the other piece of ribbon. Tie a bow with the long ends. Pin the bow in place and arrange the tails. Stitch to secure with one strand of matching thread. You are now ready to begin adding the flowers.

The roses are Spider's Webs in 4mm (⅛in) deep pink and light pink, with the deeper shade at the centre.

The irises are worked in Straight Stitches using the 7mm (¼in) apricot silk ribbon and the organdy ribbon together in the needle for the two stitches at the top of the flower. Leave the stitches rather loose so that they curve, catching them down if they need it. The lower petals are three Straight Stitches in the silk ribbon only. The bud is two Straight Stitches close together. Work two Straight Stitches around these in green ribbon for the leaves.

The fuchsias start with three loops of 4mm (⅛in) pale mauve ribbon, worked close together and stitched down with a tiny stitch on the under side of each loop. Add three small Straight Stitches at the top in 4mm (⅛in) red ribbon, leaving them rather loose.

The daisies are six Straight Stitches, worked in a circle in 4mm (⅛in) yellow ribbon. Add a green French Knot at the centre using two strands of cotton.

The violets are composed of five small Straight Stitches in 4mm (⅛in) mauve, with the two top stitches a little longer than the bottom three.

The forget-me-nots are French Knots embroidered using the 4mm (⅛in) pale blue ribbon.

The baby's breath is worked in Fly Stitches with one strand of green cotton.

DESIGN AREA

- 20cm (8in) square

MATERIALS

- 35cm (14in) square linen or linen-type fabric
- 1m x 4mm (1⅛yd x ⅛in) green double-sided satin ribbon
- 1m x 3mm (1⅛yd x ⅛in) fawn double-sided satin ribbon
- 4mm (⅛in) YLI silk ribbon: 2m (2¼yd) each of deep pink, light pink, mauve, pale blue and white; 1m (1⅛yd) each of pale mauve, red, green and yellow
- 7mm (¼in) YLI silk ribbon: 1m (1⅛yd) in apricot
- 0.5m x 9mm (½yd x ⅜in) Spark Organdy ribbon in deep apricot
- DMC Stranded Cotton: one skein each of pink, white, pale green, gold and to match fawn and green satin ribbons
- DMC Coton Perlé No 8 in deep pink
- Tracing paper, dressmaker's carbon paper
- Crewel tapestry and chenille needles
- 30cm (12in) square acid-free cardboard
- 30cm (12in) square thin batting

STITCHES USED

Straight Stitch, Fly Stitch, Herringbone Stitch, French Knot, Detached Chain, Back Stitch, Stem Stitch, Spider's Web Rose

The stitches are worked in groups and in varying lengths. Add French Knots at the tips of the stitches in one strand of white cotton.

Overcast the edge of 10cm (4in) of the white ribbon for the carnations and gather up to 5cm (2in). Fasten off the thread at the back of the work but do not cut it. Sew this end into position on the fabric (centre of the flower), then with the gathered edge facing in towards the centre, coil the ribbon around and sew down as you go. Tuck the end under the previous row and sew down.

At the top left and right of the design are two circles holding the garland. These are embroidered using two strands of gold. Work eight Detached Chain Stitches in a circular shape. Add a French Knot at the centre, and surround the circle with Back Stitches.

Work the stems of the garland in Stem Stitch with one strand of green embroidery cotton.

When your embroidery is complete, mount it over card covered with thin batting. It is then ready to frame.

DESIGN OUTLINE

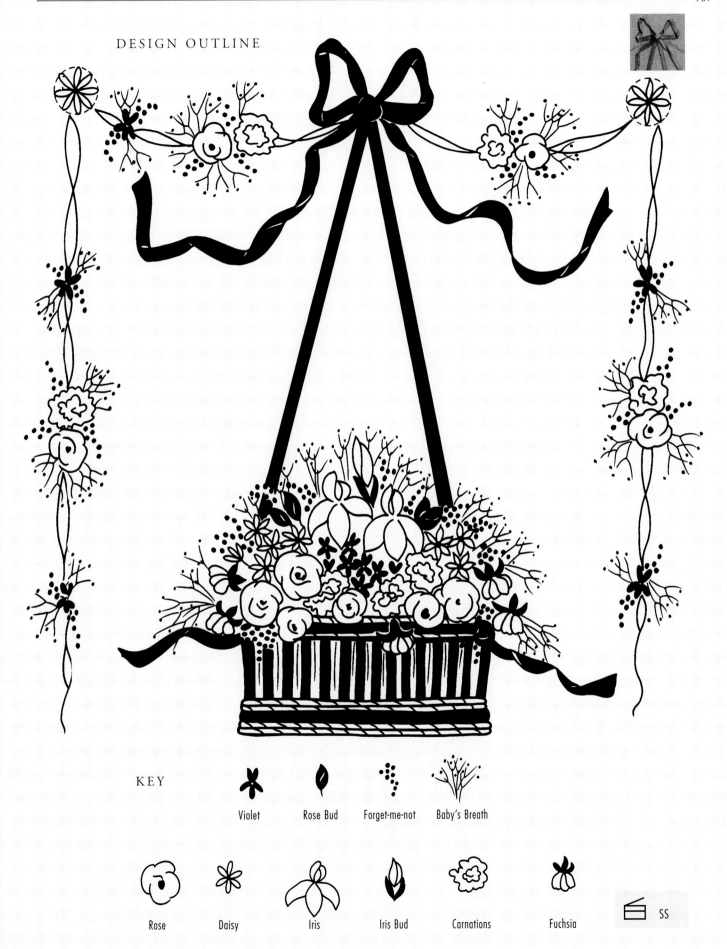

KEY

Violet   Rose Bud   Forget-me-not   Baby's Breath

Rose   Daisy   Iris   Iris Bud   Carnations   Fuchsia

SS

Field of Irises

The dark edges and variegations in the rich shades of purple,

yellow and mauve ribbons give a wonderfully

natural look to the flowers and

leaves in this simple yet effective design.

PREPARATION

Overlock the edges of your fabric. Place a piece of tracing paper over the embroidery outline on the pattern sheet and mark a dot at the centre of each iris. It is not necessary to transfer the buds, stems and leaves. When you have stitched the irises it will be easy enough to position the other elements by referring to the design. Draw an X to mark the top of the tracing. Also mark the top of the fabric.

Place the tracing on a light box and transfer the dots to the fabric with a fabric-marking pen. If your fabric is too thick to see through, make a hole at each dot, place the tracing on the right side of the fabric and mark through the holes with a fabric-marking pen.

As the irises are very close together, it could be a good idea to colour them in on the pattern sheet to make it easier to follow. If you wish, refer to the colour photograph and colour the flowers in approximately the same shades.

EMBROIDERY

NOTE: Hanah Silks are very delicate and must be handled with care. Using the large No 13 chenille needle will help to ease the ribbon through the fabric. It is recommended that you use short lengths of ribbon.

IRIS

Cut 30cm (12in) of Hanah ribbon in one of the iris colours and thread into No 13 chenille needle. Anchor the thread into the eye of the needle by stitching through it. Stitch two Ribbon Stitches side by side as shown in the Stitch Guide (page 160). Add a Ribbon Stitch on either side, starting slightly underneath the

two top petals. Droop theses petals slightly downwards.

Stitch the beard with a Lazy Daisy Stitch, making sure the ribbon is not pulled too tight.

Thread 35cm (14in) of gold 4mm (1/8in) ribbon. Knot the end of the ribbon and pull through at the centre of the iris at the top of the beard to stitch a small Ribbon Stitch for the shaft.

STEMS

Knot a 30cm (12in) length of green 7mm (1/4in) silk ribbon and thread it into a No 18 chenille needle. Pull ribbon through to the right side of the fabric, coming out underneath the centre of the beard where the stem will begin. Turn the needle clockwise, twisting the ribbon into a spiral. Pull the needle through the fabric at the desired length of the stem and anchor ribbon on wrong side of fabric.

LEAVES

Choose one of the green Hanah silks and thread a No 13 chenille needle with a 30cm (12in) length. Stitch leaves of differing lengths using Ribbon Stitch. For variation, twist the ribbon a couple of times before taking it back into the fabric.

DESIGN AREA

- 37cm x 26cm (14½in x 10¼in)

MATERIALS

- 46cm x 42cm (18in x 16½in) damask or your preferred background fabric
- Hanah Silk 15mm (⅝in) ribbon: 3m (3¼yd) each of African Violet, Lobelia, Pine Needle, Chameleon and Mossy Rock; 2.5m (2¾yd) Midas Touch; 2m (2¼yd) each of Green Apple and Wisteria
- Hanah Silk 11mm (7/16in): 2m (2¼yd) Mossy Rock
- 7mm (¼in) YLI silk ribbon: 5m (5½yd) green (72)
- 4mm (⅛in) YLI silk ribbon: 2m (2¼yd) gold (54), 4m (4⅜yd) mauve (102) and 5m (5½yd) purple (117)
- 2mm (1/16in) YLI silk ribbon: 6m (6⅝yd) grass green (20)
- No 13, 18 and 20 chenille needles
- No 8 milliner's needle
- Fabric-marking pen
- Tracing paper and fine marking pen
- Set of coloured pencils or felt-tip pens

NOTE: see pattern sheet for design

STITCHES USED

Ribbon Stitch, Lazy Daisy Stitch,
French Knot, Straight Stitch

To create the bent leaves, stitch a little more loosely than usual and catch with a single stitch of matching thread where you wish the leaf to bend.

Continue stitching in all the irises, stems and leaves, mixing the greens with the different coloured irises.

BUDS

Add some buds to match the flower heads by threading a No 13 chenille needle with a small amount of ribbon. Stitch a Ribbon Stitch in place, adding a second Ribbon Stitch that half-covers the first. Add some green either side. Stitch in the stems as before.

GRAPE HYACINTHS

Mark in the positions with a fabric pen. Refer to the key opposite for the shape of the flower head. Work double-wrap French Knots with a No 20 chenille needle and 4mm (⅛in) silk ribbon, making the knots fairly tight and close together. Work most of the knots in purple and add some in mauve in between the darker ones to shade.

STEMS AND LEAVES

With 2mm (¹⁄₁₆in) green silk ribbon in your No 20 chenille needle, add the stems, twisting them as for the iris stems. The leaves around the grape hyacinths, are worked in Straight Stitch. Place them at random, bending some of them low to the ground.

Sign and date your work for posterity.

LAUNDERING

If, when you have finished your embroidery, you feel that it needs cleaning, take it to a good drycleaner and request that it not be steamed or ironed. Hanah Silks may run if wet.

Take your finished piece to a framer experienced in framing needlework.

KEY

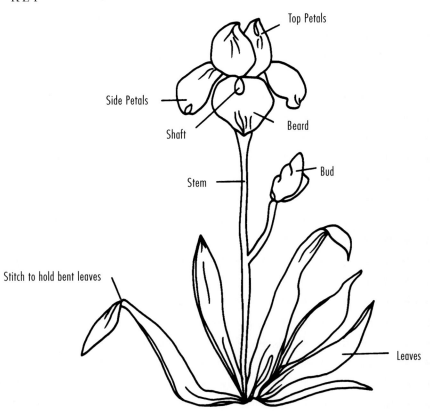

Top Petals

Side Petals

Shaft

Beard

Stem

Bud

Stitch to hold bent leaves

Leaves

IRISES

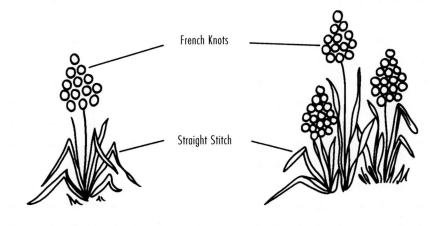

French Knots

Straight Stitch

GRAPE HYACINTHS

Peony Rose Pillow

The dusky pink hues of ribbon embroidered peony roses on soft green
dupion silk create an attractive dimension on this exquisite frilled pillow.
The technique involves stitching, twisting, wrapping and weaving
the ribbon to achieve the raised effect of fresh rose petals.

PREPARATION

Cut two pieces of the silk fabric to measure 24cm x 32cm (9½in x 12⅝in), one front and one back. Place the front piece in the embroidery hoop, select and mark the position for the roses, using the photograph as a guide.

RIBBON EMBROIDERY

To make a ribbon rose, first embroider a six-spoked web with two strands of the stranded cotton, each arm measuring 4cm (1½in) long radiating from a centre diameter of 1.3cm (½in). See Diagram 1. When stitching the web, secure the thread firmly with a Back Stitch at the beginning and the end to avoid the spokes pulling through as you work.

First Round

Thread the large-eyed needle with approximately 150cm (60in) of organza ribbon. Referring to the diagram and

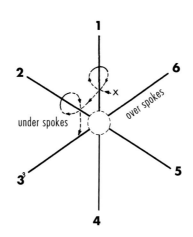

Diagram 1
Six spoke web showing direction for weaving the ribbon

working in an anti-clockwise direction, bring the needle up at the point marked X close to Spoke 1. Take the needle under Spoke 1, wrap the ribbon back over Spoke 1 and take the needle under Spoke 1 again, working all the wraps from the centre of the spoke to the outer edge. Proceed to Spoke 2, taking the needle under Spoke 2, wrapping over and under Spoke 2 as previously. Continue around the web in this manner until Spoke 6 has been completed.

DESIGN AREA

• 24cm x 32cm (9½in x 12⅝in)

MATERIALS

• 1m (1⅛yd) dupion silk

• 4.5m x 2.5cm (4⅞ yd x 1in) wide satin-edged organza ribbon [1.5m (1⅝yd) per rose]

• 3m x 4mm (3¼yd x ⅛in) old gold silk ribbon

• 3m x 7mm (3¼yd x ¼in) green silk ribbon

• Stranded cotton to match organza ribbon

• Green Kanagawa silk buttonhole twist for stems

• Nymo thread for beading

• Bronze seed beads

• No 22 tapestry needle for silk ribbon

• Large eyed needle for organza ribbon

• No 9 milliner's needle for beading

• 20cm (8in) embroidery hoop

• 250g (½lb) polyester fibrefil

STITCHES USED

Back Stitch, French Knot,
Stem Stitch, Lazy Daisy Stitch,
Straight Stitch, Ladder Stitch

Stitching, twisting and wrapping the ribbon to create the rose.

Second Round

Repeat as for first round, pushing the ribbon from the previous row down the spokes towards the centre.

Third Round

Working clockwise, bring the ribbon over the spoke (instead of under), take the needle under the spoke, then bring the ribbon over to the next spoke, all the time pushing the ribbon down the spokes to the centre. Manipulate the ribbon to form petals that will sit up on work. Refer to photograph on right.

Fourth Round

Repeat as for third round. When the round has been completed, take the thread to the back at an angle slanted back towards the rose. Thread your needle with the stranded cotton and stitch down the end of the ribbon.

Centre

Using the 4mm (⅛in) old gold ribbon and tapestry needle, fill the centre of the rose with French Knots. Fill in the spaces with bronze beads (attach the beads using Nymo thread and the No 9

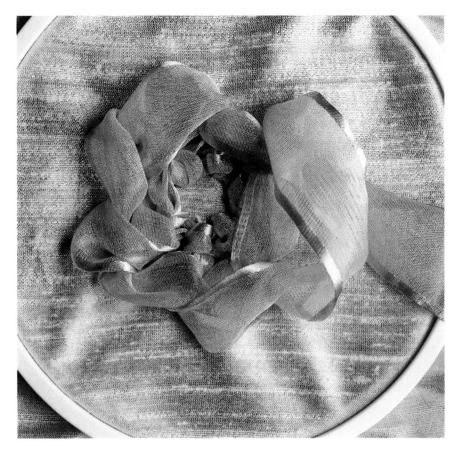

Weaving the ribbon over and under to form the petals.

Straight Stitch
in Silk Ribbon

Diagram 2
Folding the bud

milliner's needle). Make two more roses, and bead centres, following the steps already given.

To make the stems, refer to the photograph as a placement guide, then Stem Stitch trails using Kanagawa thread. Using the tapestry needle and 7mm (¼in) green silk ribbon, work leaves in Lazy Daisy Stitch.

Buds

Cut a 4mm (⅛in) length of the organza ribbon and fold to create a bud; see Diagram 2 above right. Using a length of stranded cotton and a small stitch, catch the ends of the bud at the base and stitch them into position at the tip of the stem.

Work four Straight Stitches in 7mm (¼in) green ribbon across the calyx to cover the base of the bud. Avoid pulling the ribbon too tightly.

TO MAKE UP THE PILLOW

Cut three strips of dupion silk, 25cm (10in) by the full width of the fabric. To avoid fraying, overlock or zigzag all the edges. Join the three strips into a loop. With the wrong sides together, fold in half lengthwise. Stitch three rows of gathering along the raw edges. Divide the outside edges of the pillow front evenly into two, pull up the frill to correspond, then stitch the frill to the edges of the pillow.

Lay the back pillow piece onto the front with right sides together. Stitch around leaving an opening for turning through and stuffing. Turn to the right side and fill firmlt, then Ladder Stitch the opening closed.

Stitch around, leaving an opening for adding the stuffing.

Edwardian Cottage

The delicate shading of this charming cottage and garden picture is achieved by using the modern shadow trapunto technique. The surface stitchery adds extra colour and detail to this beautiful piece.

PREPARATION

Trace the design outline from page 122 and place on a flat surface. Secure with masking tape.

Fold the fabric into quarters and finger-press to find the centre.

Centre the fabric over the pattern and secure again with masking tape.

Using the HB pencil, trace the solid line of the design lightly onto the poly-cotton fabric.

Sandwich the batting between the two layers of fabric with the traced pattern layer right side up. Tack together with long stitches in a grid formation. Refer to the step-by-step photograph.

Using one strand of medium blue green embroidery cotton in the quilting needle, stitch the design outline in a small running stitch. After stitching the design, remove the tacking stitches.

FINISHED SIZE

- 14cm x 20cm (5½in x 8in)

MATERIALS

- 2 x 35cm (14in) squares of ivory poly-cotton batiste
- 35cm (14in) square of Mountain Mist polyester batting, split in half
- DMC Tapestry Wool: one skein each of rust (7920), jade green (7861),) pale buff (7500), mushroom (7509), dark plum (7268), green (7384), deep emerald green (7385), pale mint green (7402), pale olive green (7422), blue violet (7243), rose violet (7255), white (blanc), powder blue (7800)
- DMC Broder Médicis: one skein of white (blanc)
- DMC Stranded Embroidery Cotton: one skein each of light old gold (676), light fern green (523), medium blue green (503)
- Needle Necessities Pearl Cotton No 8: overdyed pink to violet (807)
- 2mm (¹⁄₁₆in) YLI silk ribbon: 1m (1¹⁄₈yd) sage green (32)
- 4mm (¹⁄₈in) YLI silk ribbon: 1m (1¹⁄₈yd) Wedgwood blue (44), violet (101), rose violet (176)
- No 10 quilting needle
- No 20 tapestry needle
- No 7 crewel needle
- Masking tape
- HB pencil and ruler

STITCHES USED

Running Stitch, French Knot, Lazy Daisy Stitch,

Fly Stitch, Straight Stitch,

Fern Stitch, Closed Buttonhole Stitch

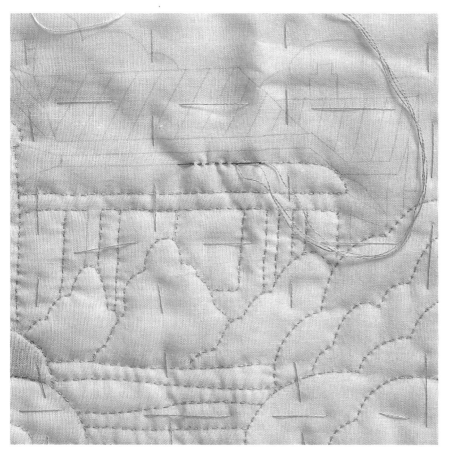

Step 1
Stitch the design outline in small running stitch.

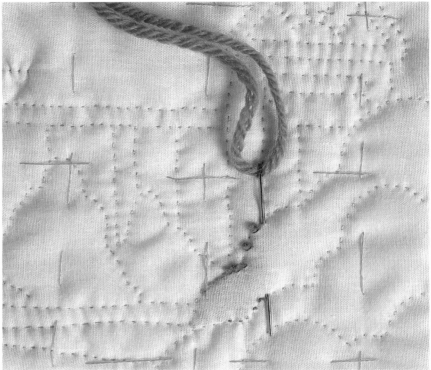

Step 2
Using double yarn, work from wrong side.

SHADOW TRAPUNTO

The shadow trapunto is worked in tapestry wool, following the colour guide on p122. Thread the tapestry needle with the appropriate colour yarn and, using the yarn double, work from wrong side. See step-by-step photograph above.

Insert the needle through the bottom layer of the fabric and the batting but do not go through the top layer. Pull the needle through so that the yarn almost disappears into the fabric. Where the needle exits the fabric, cut the yarn as close as possible being careful not to nick the fabric.

Repeat this process to fill the area of the design. The effect should be similar to a series of cut long stitches under the fabric. The yarn does not always need to run in the same direction. You might find it is sometimes easier to change the direction of stuffing to suit awkward shapes in the design.

After filling the design it is important to tuck the tiny ends of the yarn back into the fabric. Slide the needle under the back layer of fabric only, about 1cm (³⁄₈in) away from the tiny yarn ends. This will give room to swing the point of the needle which will pull or knock the tiny ends inside.

After tucking in all the ends, turn to the right side and use the point of the needle to manipulate the yarn into difficult parts of the design. Hold your work to the light to see if there are any gaps. If more stuffing is required, turn the work to the wrong side and add more yarn so it is consistent.

EMBROIDERY

All embroidery is worked using the No 7 crewel needle. Follow the Surface Embroidery Stitch and Colour Guide on

the following pages for the correct placement of stitches.

Using one strand of the Médicis wool,
stitch the fret work on the house using
French Knots and Closed Buttonhole
Stitch (see close-up above).

With two strands of stranded cotton
and one strand of silk ribbon, stitch
all the greenery using Straight Stitch,
Fern Stitch, Lazy Daisy Stitch and Fly
Stitch (see Stitch Guide page 160).

The flowers are worked using the
overdyed pearl cotton, stranded cotton
and Médicis in a combination of French
Knots, Fern Stitch, Lazy Daisy Stitch and
Straight Stitch.

When stitching the flowers in Straight
Stitch with one strand of silk ribbon, try
to keep the ribbon flat and not allow it to
twist. If it twists, the ribbon will not
spread evenly. If you make a mistake,
work another stitch over the top.

KEY
(FOR PATTERN ON PAGE 123)

o   One wrap French Knot (single stranded)

●   One wrap French Knot (double stranded)

    Lazy Daisy Stitch (single strand)

    Fly Stitch (double strand)

    Straight Stitch (double strand)

    Fern Stitch (double strand)

    Closed Buttonhole Stitch (single strand)

    Straight Stitch (silk ribbon)

DESIGN OUTLINE AND SHADOW TRAPUNTO COLOUR GUIDE

Colour Key – DMC Tapestry Wool

a = rust (7920)

b = jade green (7861)

c = pale buff (7500)

d = mushroom (7509)

e = dark plum (7268)

f = fern green (7384)

g = deep emerald (7385)

h = pale mint green (7402)

i = pale olive green (7422)

j = blue violet (7243)

k = rose violet (7255)

l = white (blanc)

m = powder blue (7800)

SURFACE EMBROIDERY DESIGN

Rose Jewellery

These delicate silk ribbon embroideries are perfectly designed for this brooch and pendant set. Quick and satisfying to create, they make a beautiful keepsake or personal gift for a special friend — with the tiny charm specially selected to give personal significance to its owner.

PREPARATION

Trace and cut out the oval template on lightweight card. Use the template to mark two oval shapes onto the template plastic and cut them out.

Draw around the plastic shapes onto the iron-on Vilene. Cut out and iron onto the reverse side of the black fabric, allowing at least 2cm (¾in) between the shapes. Transfer the outline of one oval to the front of the fabric by running a tacking thread around the edge of the Vilene shape.

EMBROIDERY

For brooch or pendant

Using fine green silk thread, work Feather Stitching as shown in Diagrams 1 and 3 on page 127. Mount fabric into hoop.

Work a single rolled rose in the position shown in Diagrams 2 and 4.

Commence with a single Colonial Knot for the centre, using the darkest shade of 4mm (⅛in) ribbon. The knot will have a better shape if the ribbon is kept flat as it is picked up on the needle and not allowed to twist or fold. Neaten the ribbon around the shaft of the needle while the needle is held in a perpendicular position in the fabric. The large

tapestry needle will give a nice cup to the centre of the knot.

Work three Whipped Stitches clockwise around the centre knot. Position the stitches as shown on the Rose diagram. Bring the needle up between the row you are working and the centre knot, halfway along the stitch just completed. Anchor each stitch into a slight curve. Numbers on the diagram denote needle movements. The needle comes up from the back of the fabric on all odd numbers and down from the front of the fabric on even numbers.

Work four or five Whipped Stitches around the previous row. Using the lighter shade of ribbon, position these stitches in the same way as in the previous row, starting each new stitch halfway back and on the inside of the previously worked stitch. Anchor each stitch into a slight curve around the previous row.

Work Straight Stitch rose buds and leaves (using green silk ribbon), positioning them as shown in Diagrams 2 or 4. Bring your needle up at the base of the bud and make a single Straight Stitch the same length as the width of the ribbon. Cover this stitch with a second Straight Stitch, starting immediately below and extending just beyond the tip of the first stitch. Using a single strand of cotton, come up at the base of the bud and take a single Straight Stitch two-thirds of the way up the centre of the Ribbon Stitch. Work a Fly Stitch around the bud, anchoring

DESIGN AREA

- 10cm x 5cm (4in x 2in) for each piece

MATERIALS

- 2m x 4mm (2¼yd x ⅛in) silk ribbon in two shades of the chosen colour
- 1m x 2mm (1⅛yd x 1⁄16in) silk ribbon in green
- DMC Coton Perlé 8 for edge stitching brooch or pendant
- 20cm x 12cm (8in x 4¾in) black silk fabric
- Kanagawa No 50 silk, or machine embroidery thread, in green
- DMC Stranded Embroidery Cotton in cream
- 10cm x 5cm (4in x 2in) of template plastic
- 10cm x 5cm (4in x 2in) of Iron-on Vilene
- 10cm x 5cm (4in x 2in) of Soft-Sew Vilene
- 60cm (24in) chain, for pendant, or brooch pin
- Small charm of your choice
- 7cm (2¾in) spring embroidery hoop
- Large tapestry needle

NOTE: see p127 for templates and stitch key. To thread the ribbon, pass it through the eye of the needle and then put needle through the short end of the ribbon about 12mm (½in) from the beginning. Pull back on the long end of the ribbon until the ribbon locks firmly into the eye of the needle. To start a stitch, leave a small tail hanging at the back of the work. Pierce this tail as the first stitch is taken. To finish a ribbon, weave in behind the stitching, if possible, or cut off leaving a tail to be caught in as the next thread is started.

STITCHES USED

Colonial Knot, Straight Stitch,
Feather Stitch, Whipped Stitch, Fly Stitch,
Ladder Stitch, Palestrina Stitch

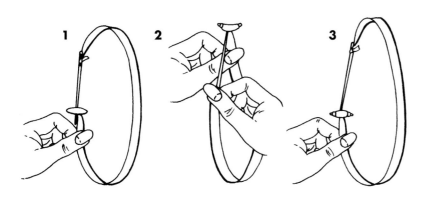

Whipped Stitch

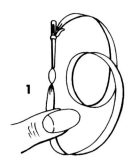

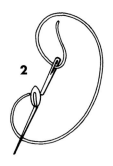

Rose Bud

it with a tiny Straight Stitch or use this thread to form a stem for the bud.

Finish the design by scattering Colonial Knots in two strands of DMC cream or tiny beads through the design. Stitch on selected charm.

ASSEMBLY

Cut a piece of Soft-Sew Vilene to fit each of the plastic shapes. Cut out the Vilene backed ovals (one embroidered, one plain), allowing 6mm (¼in) turnings beyond the edge of the Vilene backing. Using strong thread, work a row of gathering stitches around each fabric oval 3mm (⅛in) outside the Vilene edge. Pull up over the padded plastic shapes and fasten securely. Place the two ovals wrong sides together and Ladder Stitch together securely. Using two strands of Perlé 8, work a row of Palestrina Stitch around the edge of the oval, catching the fabric of the front and back discs each time a new stitch is started (points B and C on the Palestrina Stitch Diagram).

Sew on brooch back, or a jewellery finding to the top of the pendant for a chain. To edge with a chain as shown in the photograph, omit the Palestrina Stitch edging, find the centre of the chain and pin or tack the chain in place around the edge, pulling the chain together at the top of the oval. Check to make sure the pendant is centred correctly before stitching the chain in place with the matching coloured thread.

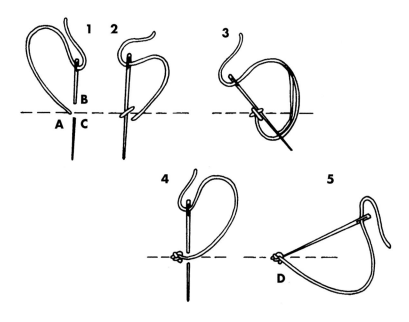

Palestrina Stitch

TEMPLATE

PENDANT

Diagram 1   Diagram 2

KEY

   Roses

   Rose Buds

o   Colonial Knots

   Leaves

BROOCH

Diagram 3   Diagram 4

ROSE

 SS

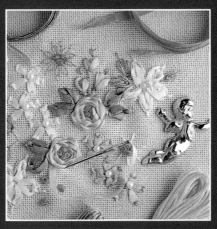

From Times Past

*Relive the beauty and appeal of yesteryear
using these projects and ideas to further your
own appreciation for and enjoyment
of ribbon embroidery.*

Memories

Sentimental treasures, scraps of lace, sepia photographs
and silk ribbon embroidery — memories are made of these.
This superb montage was inspired by the Guardian Angel and card
given by the bride as a thankyou to her bridesmaid.

PREPARATION

Centre your handkerchief (or whatever you wish to use) on your square of backing fabric. Stitch down closely around the edges, particularly around any lace. If you are using old linen, you may find it is slightly out of shape. Do not let this deter you, this is part of its appeal.

Mark the position of the main photo and card, lightly trace around the edges in pencil to use as a guide. The photos/card will not be placed until the piece is nearly finished.

Stitch down the various laces and

motifs. Remember to also catch down the outer edge of the lace. See Diagram 1.

For the oval frame of the small picture, trace the template (Diagram 2) and cut from template plastic or cardboard. If using plastic, hold the scissors still and turn the plastic around as you cut; this will ensure a smoother outline than if you move the scissors around as you are cutting.

Glue one end of the coffee silk ribbon (66) to the plastic template and commence binding the ribbon very evenly (at an angle) around the oval shape. Glue the end on the same side as you started.

Cut a photo to fit the ribbon covered frame. Glue the frame onto the photo. Position the oval frame on your fabric and trace the position of the bottom outline of the frame.

EMBROIDERY

Mark in the position of the roses. Using No 24 chenille needle and thread to match the silk ribbon, work the spokes of the web approximately 7mm (¼in) long (finished rose is approximately 2cm

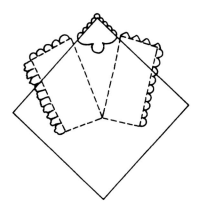

Diagram 1
Position of handkerchief and lace with marked photo outlines.

DESIGN AREA

- 50cm (19¾in) square

MATERIALS

- 50cm (½yd) square backing fabric (furnishing fabric is a good weight)
- Sepia photographs
- Guardian Angel and card (available from gift shops)
- Old or new handkerchief with one lacy corner
- 3 x decorative buttons with shanks
- 2 x decorative flat buttons
- 2 x brass heart charms
- Scraps of old or new lace and lace motifs (tea or coffee dyed)
- Any other mementos such as earrings, brooches, bracelets, etc
- Tiny glass beads in gold or brown
- Madeira Silk thread: one skein each of gold (2208), brown (2113), ecru
- 7mm (¼in) YLI silk ribbon: 4m (4⅜yd) each of coffee (66), pale coffee (51) and cream (34)
- No 24 chenille needle
- No 10 crewel needle
- Double-sided, acid-free tape
- 12.5cm (5in) square of template plastic or cardboard
- Pencil

NOTE: this is an inspirational project designed to give you ideas for your own design to commemorate a special event. You may choose to use more photographs or less, include the Guardian Angel and card or some other theme. The combination of elements is limited only by your imagination.

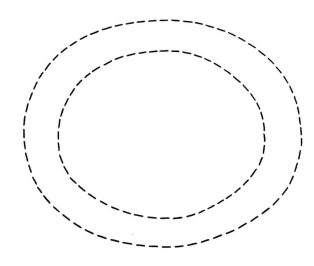

Diagram 2
Oval photo frame template.

STITCHES USED

Spider's Web Rose, Ribbon Stitch,
French Knot, Back Stitch

(¾in) diameter). Refer to the step-by-step photograph below and Spider's Web Rose diagram in Stitch Guide p160. Work the ribbon roses with single twist French Knot centres. Add the Ribbon Stitch leaves. See the main photograph for colour placement. Work ribbon roses and leaves between the markings for photos.

Changing to No 10 crewel needle and one strand of gold Madeira Silk thread, embroider five French Knots (two twists around the needle) close together in a circle for the forget-me-not flowers. Add a French Knot in brown at the centre of each flower. The Buds are French Knots in one strand of gold thread (two twists graduating out to one twist at the very tip of the spray).

Using ecru Madeira Silk, work French Knots at random around the design. Stitch on the small gold hearts, tucking the tops under the roses.

With a double strand of cotton, stitch the three main buttons (with shanks) closely together into position. See Diagram 3.

Using the double-sided tape, adhere the photos into position. Place the tape as close to the edges as possible and fill the central area with strips of tape as well. Tape the back of the oval and then place it in position over the photos with the bottom edge tucked under the silk roses.

Stitch tiny beads at random through the embroidery. Using a double strand of cotton, stitch the two flat buttons into position, stitching through the photo and card.

Using the chenille needle and ribbon, work French Knots around the group of buttons to fill in any gaps. See photograph below for suggested placement.

Stitch any extra motifs, buttons, or whatever you choose into position. If you are using something similar to the bracelet, make sure you stitch it securely along the entire length, say on every sec-

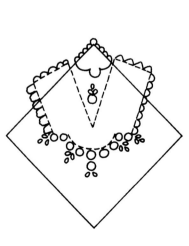

Diagram 3
Embroidery and button placement

ond link, to distribute the weight evenly. Remember it is all right to stitch through the photo and card. It will help to keep the whole assembly secure.

✂ **HELPFUL HINT**

Stitch down items rather than gluing. The photos/card are adhered to the fabric with double-sided, acid-free tape and stitched at the corners. Glue may pucker the fabric when dried and your work will be spoilt.

Embroider your name and any other details around the bottom edge of the handkerchief in tiny Back Stitches.

FRAMING

❖

Your montage should be professionally framed. Ask the framer to construct a box frame so that the glass will protect your treasured memories.

Lady Dreaming in the Garden

*The very picture of romance, this nostalgic embroidery has
been stitched on a printed silk panel with roses, daisies,
foxgloves, columbines and more, worked in delicately shaded
silk ribbon and stranded cotton.*

PREPARATION

Hand overcast or machine overlock the raw edges of the silk panel. If you prefer to work on a frame, a tapestry frame large enough to expose the entire print is the most suitable. Using a round wooden frame is not recommended as it may damage the print.

To mount the print in the frame, machine stitch a strip of fabric to the top and bottom of the print and attach the fabric to the frame. Do not stitch the actual silk to the frame as it may pull when the tension is tightened.

EMBROIDERY

There are no hard and fast rules on how much or how little embroidery you should add to the silk panel. The instruc-

tions are given as a guide to follow or alter as you wish.

Refer to the colour photograph, flower placement guide and table on page 138 and 139. The table gives colours, stitches and needles for each element of the design.

FOR THE HAT

Make three tiny Folded Ribbon Roses with 7mm (¼in) dusky pink using the darker shade for centres. Work tiny Ribbon Stitch leaves in 4mm (⅛in) blue-green and dark blue-green. Add some dusky pink ribbon French Knot rosebuds.

Using one strand of dusky pink stranded cotton, Stem Stitch around the brim of the hat, and in the folds of the dress. Also stitch the middle seam of the right sleeve, from the top to half-way down. Buttonhole Stitch the collar and hem of the dress, also using pink. The Petticoat is Buttonhole Stitched in one strand of white.

The lady's sash is stitched with 7mm (¼in) mauve silk ribbon, using Ribbon Stitch. Work a Bullion Rose in the centre of the sash using No 7 milliner's needle and one strand of darker pink for the centre and the lighter pink to highlight the outside petals.

The climbing roses are worked in Ribbon Stitch with the centres in the darkest dusky pink, shading out to the lightest. Allow the outer petals to remain loose and work some petals curving around the side and some facing downwards. The stems are Stem Stitched in one strand of dark leaf green thread. Add small Ribbon Stitch leaves in blue-green and dark blue-green. Don't forget to stitch the rose in the lady's hand.

The trailing daisies are worked in Ribbon Stitch using pinkish-beige ribbon for the five petals and adding a gold ribbon French Knot for the centre. Add the leaves in Ribbon Stitch using grass green ribbon and stitch some Ribbon Stitch small buds and French Knots in

FINISHED SIZE

- 27cm x 19cm (10½in x 7½in)

MATERIALS

- Lady Dreaming in the Garden printed silk panel

- 13mm (½in) YLI silk ribbon: 1m (1⅛yd) cream (156)

- 7mm (¼in) YLI silk ribbon: 0.5m (½yd) each of medium dusky pink (158), dark dusky pink (159); 1m (1⅛yd) of mauve (179), 2m (2¼yd) of forest green (21)

- 4mm (⅛in) YLI silk ribbon: 1m (1⅛yd) each of medium dusky pink (158), dark dusky pink (159), gold (78), rose pink (112), medium rose pink (113), dark rose pink (114), pale soft pink (5), soft pink (8), cream (156), purple (177), violet (85), green (171); 2m (2¼yd) each of dusky pink (157), blue-green (32), dark blue-green (33), pinkish-beige (65), grass green (72), lemon (14)

- Kacoonda silk ribbon: 2m x 4mm (2¼yd x ⅛in) variegated blue/lavender/yellow (3c)

- Anchor Stranded Cotton: one skein each of white, dusky pink (893), dark dusky pink (895), dark olive green (681), dark leaf green (263), orange-yellow (303), tan/brown (339)

- No 7 milliner's needle

- No 18, 20, 22 chenille needles

- Tapestry frame (optional)

STITCHES USED

Folded Ribbon Rose, Ribbon Stitch, Buttonhole Stitch, Stem Stitch, Straight Stitch, French Knot, Couching, Bullion Stitch

1. Fold raw edge down a little then roll ribbon three or four times to form centre of rose. Secure with three or four stitches.

3. Pull centre of the rose down so when you roll it into the ribbon it will be level with the top of the fold. Stitch the base of the rose after each fold.

Folded Ribbon Rose

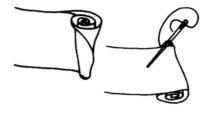

2. Fold ribbon on the cross. Each fold of ribbon is a petal.

4. Keep folding and stitching until you have the size and shape you want. To finish, stitch the ribbon at the bottom of the rose to prevent fraying.

the pinkish-beige ribbon. The stems are couched in dark olive green thread.

Draw in five stems for the foxgloves. Starting from the top of each stem and using the darkest colour first, stitch a couple of French Knots then continue with two Ribbon Stitches stitched close together for the flower.

Continue stitching in the flowers down the stem by adding an extra petal in a fan shape until there are four or five petals. Graduate the colours from darkest to lightest as you work down the stem. Stitch the foxglove leaves using 7mm (¼in) ribbon and Ribbon Stitch. Place a Straight Stitch with two strands of green in the centre of some of the leaves. With stranded cotton, stitch in the stems, adding a few French Knots at the very top.

The arum lilies are Ribbon Stitched with 13mm (½in) cream ribbon. Using two strands of orange-yellow stranded cotton, place a 12-wrap Bullion Stitch at

the centre of each lily. Add the leaves around the bottom using 7mm (¼in) forest green ribbon.

Work the heartsease in the lower left-hand corner. Using the purple ribbon, stitch two Ribbon Stitches at the top of the flower. With the cream ribbon, add two side petals and then three lemon petals at the base of the flower. With one strand of tan/brown thread, work some Straight Stitches in the side and lower petals. Stitch the stems in place with two strands of green and work the leaves in three Straight Stitches, angling the two side stitches slightly outwards. Add a couple of buds by working a purple Ribbon Stitch and partially covering it with a lemon petal.

The violets beneath the deeper pink foxgloves are worked next. With purple ribbon, stitch five Ribbon Stitch petals – two at the top and three at the bottom. Add a French Knot in the centre in the gold ribbon. Stem Stitch the stems and work the leaves with two strands of green, using Buttonhole Stitch in the shape of a heart.

Beneath the pale pink foxgloves, work some more violets using the variegated Kacoonda ribbon. Add leaves and stems as before. Finally, work the columbines with three petals in lemon ribbon, then stitch a petal either side and in the middle of these, using the variegated ribbon. Add the curls at the top by stitching through a very short piece of lemon ribbon to secure it, then twisting it tightly before pulling through to the back. Catch the curl with a stitch to hold it in place. Stem Stitch the stems and add the Ribbon Stitch leaves in the shape of a fan.

You may choose to add some more small French Knot flowers and Lazy Daisy leaves around the base of the embroidery if you wish.

Your completed embroidery can be professionally framed in a box frame or made up into a cushion.

SUBJECT	STITCH	THREAD/RIBBON	NEEDLE
Roses on Hat	Folded Ribbon Roses	7mm (¼in) dusky pink (158 & 159)	No 7 milliner's
Sash	Ribbon Stitch	7mm (¼in) mauve (179)	No 18 chenille
Dress Outline	Buttonhole and Stem Stitch	Anchor pink (893), and tan/brown (339), one strand	No 7 milliner's
Climbing Roses	Ribbon Stitch	4mm (⅛in) dusky pinks (157,158,159)	No 20 chenille
Leaves	Ribbon Stitch	4mm (⅛in) blue-green (32 & 33)	No 20 chenille
Trailing Daisies	Ribbon Stitch	4mm (⅛in) pinkish-beige (65)	No 18 chenille
Centres	French Knots	4mm (⅛in) gold (78)	No 22 chenille
Leaves	Ribbon Stitch	4mm (⅛in) grass green (72)	No 20 chenille
Stems	Couching	Anchor dark olive green (681), two strands	No 7 milliner's
Foxgloves	Ribbon Stitch	4mm (⅛in) rose pinks (112, 113 & 114), soft pinks (5 & 8)	No 18 chenille
Leaves	Ribbon Stitch	7mm (¼in) forest green (21)	No 18 chenille
Stems	Stem Stitch	Anchor dark leaf green (263)	No 7 milliner's
Arum Lilies	Ribbon Stitch	13mm (½in) cream (156)	No 18 chenille
Centres	Bullion Stitch	Anchor orange-yellow (303)	No 7 milliner's
Leaves	Ribbon Stitch	7mm (¼in) forest green (21)	No 18 chenille
Heartsease	Ribbon Stitch	4mm (⅛in) lemon (14), & 4mm (⅛in) cream (156)	No 18 chenille
		4mm (⅛in) purple (177), Anchor tan/brown (339), one strand	No 7 milliner's
Leaves/stems	Stem Stitch and Straight Stitch	Anchor dark leaf green (263), two strands	No 7 milliner's
Violets	Ribbon Stitch	4mm (⅛in) violet (85) and 4mm (⅛in) variegated (3c)	No 18 chenille
Centres	French Knots	4mm (⅛in) gold (78)	No 22 chenille
Leaves	Buttonhole Stitch	Anchor dark olive green (263), one strand	No 7 milliner's
Columbines	Ribbon Stitch	4mm (⅛in) lemon (14) and 4mm (⅛in) variegated (3c)	No 18 chenille
Leaves	Ribbon Stitch	4mm (⅛in) green (171)	No 20 chenille

FLOWER
PLACEMENT GUIDE

Trailing Daisies

Climbing Roses

Foxgloves

Heartsease

Columbines

Violets

Arum Lilies

105%

Victorian Scissors Case and Pincushion

Reminiscent of the sewing accessories favoured by ladies of the Victorian era, this exquisite set is both beautiful and useful. It was designed using silk ribbon and silk thread on a background of gold silk damask.

SCISSORS CASE

There are four pieces in the scissors case cardboard kit: two thick outers and two thin liners. Using a light coat of spray adhesive, fix both the thick pieces and the taller thin piece to a layer of batting and cut out.

NOTE: the shorter thin cardboard piece is not padded.

Place both thin cardboard pieces on the lining fabric and cut out, leaving a 12mm (1/2in) seam allowance all around. Using a double thread, sew a small running stitch around the edge of both fabric pieces and gather up firmly over the cardboard. If necessary, make a couple of large stitches across the back of the piece to keep the sides held firmly together.

Lay the taller thick piece on the wrong side of the silk damask. Cut out leaving approximately 12mm (1/2in) seam allowance all around. Again, use a double thread to work Running Stitch around the edge and gather firmly over cardboard and batting.

Take the smaller thick cardboard piece and place on the wrong side of the silk damask.

Trace around the shape using the fading marker pen. Tack over the marked line and also down the centre of the shape. Turn to right side.

NOTE: this piece is not cut out. It needs to remain on a larger piece of fabric so it can be put in a small hoop.

EMBROIDERY

GATHERED ROSES, BUDS AND LEAVES

Using the pattern as a guide, mark the centre of each gathered rose with a dot. Thread a 25cm (10in) length of Petals red wine ribbon into No 18 chenille needle. Commencing at the end opposite

FINISHED SIZE

- CASE: 10cm x 7cm (4in x 2¾in)
- PINCUSHION: 9.5cm (3¾in)

MATERIALS

- 30cm (12in) square gold silk damask or similar fabric
- 20cm (8in) square of gold silk lining fabric
- 7mm (1/4in) Petals silk ribbon: one skein each of red wine and hunter green
- 7mm (1/4in) YLI silk ribbon: 2m (2¼yd) pale yellow (12)
- 4mm (1/8in) YLI silk ribbon: 2m (2¼yd) deep dusty pink (159), 4m (4⅜yd) grey green (33)
- Madeira silk thread: one packet each of grey green (1704), steel grey (1707), gold (2013)
- Mill Hill Glass Seed Beads: one packet each of gold and burgundy (02012)
- Scissors case cardboard kit
- Piece of thin batting
- Spray adhesive
- Jo Sonja's gold paint (optional)
- Liner brush
- Small hoop
- No 18 and 22 chenille needles
- Beading needle
- No 8 crewel needle
- Doll or bear making needle
- Fading marker pen
- Gold machine thread

For cords and tassels:

- YLI 1000 denier thread: one skein each of deep cardinal red (2), old gold (814), burgundy (135)
- Small amount DMC light gold Metallic Floss
- Beads of your choice (optional)
- Sawdust or wool stuffing

STITCHES USED

French Knot, Straight Stitch, Split Stitch,
Ribbon Stitch, Running Stitch

to the needle, work a line of Running Stitches with crewel needle and matching machine thread along the lower edge of the ribbon. Secure the thread at the beginning but do not end off. Remove the crewel needle and cut excess thread.

With the ribbon still threaded into the chenille needle, pass the ribbon up through the fabric at the centre dot of a rose. Leave just a small tail hanging on the wrong side of the fabric which should be secured.

Again, thread the crewel needle with matching machine thread. Then, using the gathering thread, gently pull up the silk ribbon closest to the fabric end. Take the ribbon around in a small circle, securing at intervals with invisible stitches using the crewel needle. Keep circling the ribbon around in circles until approximately a needle's length from the end of the ribbon. Pass the chenille needle through to the back of the fabric. Secure and cut ribbon. Repeat these steps for the other two gathered roses.

Gently open the gathers to find the centre of the flower. Using one strand of Madeira gold silk (2013) thread in your No 8 crewel needle, make approximately seven or eight French Knots.

Around each rose, work three or four rosebuds in the Petals red wine silk ribbon, each consisting of two 'puffy' Straight Stitches.

For the Rose Leaves

Thread No 18 chenille needle with Petals hunter green ribbon. Surround the roses and buds with leaves as desired using Ribbon Stitch. Use the pattern as a guide but there is no need to follow it leaf for leaf. All pieces should have their own 'personality'. Just remember to keep within the tacked area.

Berry Sprays

Using your crewel or beading needle, attach three gold 4mm (¹⁄₈in) beads around your roses in three different areas. Use machine thread for this and see diagram on page 145 for placement.

Thread your chenille needle with a piece of 7mm (¼in) pale yellow (12). Cover each bead with a tight Ribbon Stitch. The ribbon should cover the bead easily. If, however, the stitch slides to the side, add another stitch.

Thread the No 22 chenille needle with 4mm (¹⁄₈in) deep dusty pink (159) silk ribbon. Surround the berries with a Ribbon Stitch to each side. If you wish to highlight the covered beads, touch each with a little watered-down gold paint and liner brush.

Using the pattern on page 145 as a guide, carefully draw or trace the stems on to the fabric. Take one strand each of silk thread grey green (1704) and steel grey (1707). Thread together into your crewel needle. Work the stems in a small Split Stitch, taking care not to exceed the tacked borderline.

Add tiny Ribbon Stitch leaves in 4mm (⅛in) grey green (33). Finish with gold and burgundy beads at the stem ends.

Now the embroidery is complete, cut around the tacked shape leaving a 12mm (½in) seam allowance and remove all the tacking stitches. As before, sew a running stitch around the edge of the shape and gather up the fabric over the padded cardboard shape.

ASSEMBLY

Take the smaller liner piece and the embroidered front piece and slip stitch both pieces together. Repeat with the two large pieces. Place both pieces together and run a final slip stitch around the edge to join.

Twisted Cord

Cut three 125cm (49in) lengths each of YLI Silk 1000 Denier deep cardinal red (2) and burgundy (135), two of old gold (814) and one length of DMC gold Metallic Floss.

Stretch the threads tightly and, with a friend, twist the threads in opposite directions until you feel a resistance. Find the centre of the thread. Fold in half and, holding the ends firmly, gradually let the cord go. Secure the end by rolling sticky tape tightly around the threads.

Starting with the folded end of the cord and at centre bottom of the scissors case, attach the cord using matching thread, laying the sewing thread along the twists so they will not be seen.

Make a loop at the top of the scissors case and continue down the other side until you reach the beginning.

The end of the cord can be threaded into your chenille needle and threaded in between the back and front of the scissors case to disappear inside.

Tassels

Cut a 150cm (59in) length of each of the three silk threads and the gold DMC thread. Wind the four threads together around a piece of card measuring 5cm (2in). Pass an extra piece of silk thread through the tassel, slide to the top and knot tightly. Slide tassel off card. Thread a needle with a length of silk thread and take a small double stitch in the side of the tassel.

Wrap the thread around the tassel to make the neck. Pass the needle under the wraps and up through the centre of the tassel. Turn the needle and take the thread back down through the centre of the tassel and out at the bottom. Cut tassel to even.

If you wish, a number of beads can be threaded onto the tassel before it is attached to the cord at the base of the scissors case.

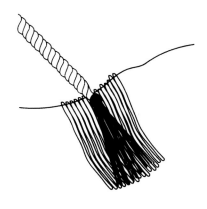

Tassel
Place knotted cord over tassel threads. Gently nestle the cord within the threads. Tie above knot.

Silk ribbon embroidery was very popular during Victorian times with both professional and amateur embroiderers alike. They used ribbon embroidery on pincushions, workbags, pocketbooks and lids for sewing boxes. The colours used were very bright and flowers were a popular theme. Stitches were very simple, including Straight Stitch, French Knot, Lazy Daisy and Satin Stitch. Another stunning effect was created by cutting silk gauze and folding it to make large diaphonous flowers and roses.

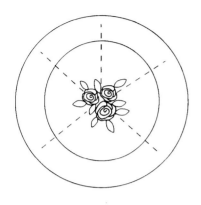

Pincushion Diagram
Divide pincushion into five equal sections and tack to mark each section. Embroider to each side of the tacked lines.

PINCUSHION

Cut two circles of silk damask 14cm (5½in) in diameter and zigzag the edges. Set aside one piece for the back. Find the centre of the front circle and, using the pattern as a guide, mark in the centres of the gathered roses. Work the embroidery design as instructed for the scissors case, but this time following a circular pattern.

After the rose embroidery has been completed, place the fabric piece flat on the table and mark five equal sections with pins. Tack along these lines and continue the smaller embroidery, making sure not to embroider along these lines. Refer to diagram.

When the embroidery is complete, take both circles and, with right sides together, machine-stitch around leaving a 1cm (⅜in) seam allowance and a small opening to turn through. Turn right side out, fill with sawdust or wool stuffing and stitch opening closed.

Make a twisted cord as directed for scissors case, but cut the lengths to 80cm (31½in). Stitch this cord to the seamline around the pincushion, hiding the end beneath the beginning of the cord.

Take a long double length of 1000 Denier silk old gold (814) and thread into a doll or bearmaking needle. Make a small double stitch in the centre base of the pincushion, come up through the centre of the cushion and lay along tacked lines, coming up through the centre again until the pincushion is divided into equal sections. The thread needs to be pulled gently but firmly to shape the cushion into equal sections. Finish with a small double stitch beneath an embroidered flower.

Make another twisted cord, using the same number and colours of threads but measuring 38cm (15in) in length. Twist and fold in two to make a cord, but this time make a knot in the cord approximately 11cm (4½in) from the folded end of the cord.

Make a tassel as instructed for the scissors case and pass the silk thread through the wraps. This time slide the tassel off the card without tying at the top. Place the knotted end of the cord on top of the tassel threads and gently nestle it within the threads. Tie above the knot. Make neck of tassel as instructed for scissors case. Trim tassel ends.

EMBROIDERY PLACEMENT GUIDE

SCISSORS CASE

PINCUSHION

SS

Lady with Bonnet

*This charming picture of a fashionably dressed woman is mounted on
a silk print of an antique photo album page. The print has been embellished
with thread embroidery, silk and organdy ribbons and lace medallions.
This can also be used as inspiration for your own phototgraphs.*

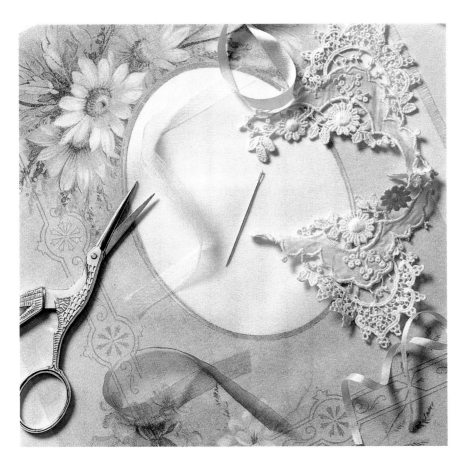

FINISHED SIZE

- 24cm x 18cm (9½in x 7in)

MATERIALS

- Lady with Bonnet silk print

- Daisy photo mount silk print

- DMC Stranded Embroidery Cotton: one skein each of ultra very light beige brown (543), medium yellow green (3347), very dark grape (3802), medium caramel (3827), medium pine green (3363)

- Petals 7mm (¼in) silk ribbon: 1m (1⅛yd) each of Peace, French Lace, Blue Pine and Mint Julep

- Petals 4mm (⅛in) silk ribbon: 1m (1⅛yd) French Lace

- YLI 9mm (⅜in) organdy ribbon: 1m (1⅛yd) each of white (1), pale grey (39), grey/brown (56), dark green (32)

- Mokuba 9mm (⅜in) organdy ribbon: 1m (1⅛yd) old gold (14)

- Two lace medallions

- No 18 and 20 chenille needle

- No 7 milliner's needle

STITCHES USED

Ribbon Stitch, Side Ribbon Stitch,

French Knot, Stem Stitch

PREPARATION

Overlock the edges of the Daisy Print to prevent fraying.

Leaving a 3mm (⅛in) seam allowance, cut carefully around the oval edge of the Lady with Bonnet print. Arrange the print inside the picture frame oval of the Daisy Print and tack in position with small stitches. These tacking stitches will remain in place.

Arrange the lace medallions at the top and bottom of the Lady with Bonnet print and attach them through both prints, using stab stitches. Make sure the lace is firmly attached and sits flat on the prints.

EMBROIDERY

NOTE: sew down all ribbon ends on the back of the work as it progresses so that the loose ends do not get in the way and come through to the front of the work.

Lady with Bonnet

Cut 30cm (12in) of 4mm (⅛in) Petals French Lace silk ribbon and thread a No 20 chenille needle. Stitch through the ribbon to secure it at the eye of the needle. Sew Ribbon Stitches around the oval shape of the Lady with Bonnet print from the bottom of the print to the top. Refer to the close-up photograph and work the stitches on the angle shown, following the shape of the oval. The stitches should be worked close together to cover the raw edge of the print.

Sew seven evenly-spaced French Knots using 4mm (⅛in) French Lace silk ribbon up the centre of each side of the print to emphasise the picture frame border.

The background of the print is then filled in with French Knots, using two strands of DMC 543 and a No 7 milliner's needle. Start on one side of the picture and work from the bottom to the top, using the picture and the frame as the outline. Work around the lace medallions, then when the first side is completed, start the second side, working from the bottom to the top in the same manner. Place the knots very close together so that they form a textured frame for the picture.

When this has been completed, use 7mm (¼in) French Lace silk ribbon to embroider Ribbon Stitches (angled as before) around the outside edge of the picture frame.

Daisy Print

Select yellow and cream sections of the 7mm (¼in) Peace silk ribbon and use these as the predominant colours when stitching the daisies. A hint of lightly shaded pink is effective if used in the centres of the petals, shading out to yellow at the tips.

Start with the full daisy in the centre. Work loose Ribbon Stitches and Side Ribbon Stitches (work as for Ribbon Stitch, but instead of taking the needle through the centre of the ribbon, take to one side) following the petals on the print. When these have been completed and the loose ends are stitched down on the back of the embroidery, work Ribbon Stitches in pale grey organdy ribbon underneath and inside the top five com-

pleted daisy petals. Allow the organdy to show on the sides of the petals, as if they are extra petals between and behind the silk ribbon ones. Stitch the organdy ribbon ends down on the back of the work to prevent fraying and to keep the work firm.

When the petals of the centre daisy are complete, work the left hand daisy in the same manner. This time, however, use 7mm (¼in) Peace silk ribbon on the left-hand side of the daisy and shade this into 7mm (¼in) Mint Julep ribbon on the right side. When shading in between the petals, use white organdy in the lightest part of the flower and shade it around to the right side where pale grey organdy is used. A few of the petals of this daisy have to be placed between those of the centre daisy.

The daisy on the right side of the print is embroidered in the same manner as the centre daisy. This time use the 7mm (¼in) Mint Julep ribbon and shadow the petals with the old gold organdy ribbon.

When the three daisies have been completed, the centres are worked with French Knots using two strands of DMC thread – use 3802 nearest the petals and work areas of 3347, 3827 and 3363 into the centre.

The side view daisy on the left is embroidered in Ribbon Stitch, using only organdy ribbon. Start with the pale grey at the top and stitch one or two petals in each shade – grey brown and old gold, with the dark green at the bottom.

Finally, the daisy leaves are stitched in 7mm (¼in) Blue Pine silk ribbon. Stitch two leaves at the bottom of the centre daisy flower. Loose Ribbon Stitch is used and the point of the leaf is embroidered first, followed by stitches alternating to the left and right until each leaf is completed. Then, using two strands of DMC 3363, embroider the centre and side veins of the leaves in Stem Stitch.

FRAMING

Don't forget to sign your work. The embroidery needs to be professionally framed by a framer who is experienced in framing fabrics. A box frame will need to be constructed to preserve the silk and protect the raised embroidery.

HELPFUL HINT

Use of an embroidery hoop with the silk prints is not recommended as the hoop will leave marks which are difficult to remove. To avoid puckering the print, ensure that your stitches are not pulled too tightly.

Nostalgic Picture Frame

*A fitting presentation for a treasured image or
a favourite text, this romantic picture is decorated
with guipure lace motifs, vintage silk ribbon flowers
and a tiny heart charm.*

PREPARATION

Referring to the close-up photograph, position the lace motifs on the picture mount. Place the smaller motif in the upper left corner of the opening. Curve the larger motif around the lower right corner. Glue carefully into position, using spots of glue on a toothpick and ensuring that no glue is visible on the mount. If desired, the daisies at the top of the large motif can be cut out and repositioned. You might choose to cut out the single daisy at the left and position it above the two daisies at the top of the motif.

FLOWERS AND LEAVES

You will require five medium-sized scalloped flowers with twisted centres and seven buds. These flowers and buds are made by combining the Hanah and Vintage silk ribbons as you wish for the centres and the outer petals. You will also need three leaves made from 22mm (⁷⁄₈in) green ribbon and eight looped leaves made from 4mm (¹⁄₈in) ribbon.

Scalloped Flowers with Twisted Centres

Insert the ends of the wire loop into the holes at the top of the Vintage Rose Spindle. Pass the end of the ribbon through the wire loop, left to right (if left-handed, work in the reverse direction), as shown in photograph on page 153. Turn down the end of the ribbon at a 45-degree angle. Pass the folded tail back to the left side, holding the ribbon in your left hand. Turn the spindle towards you, winding the ribbon three times around the wire loop to form the centre of the flower. Stitch to hold the roll in place. Cut off the thread.

Holding the ribbon between your thumb and forefinger (with your thumb underneath), fold the ribbon away from the centre roll, turning the top edge of the ribbon to the base of the flower at the centre back. Turn the spindle with your other hand at the same time, pinching the base of the flower with your fingers to hold. Continue folding and turning until you have formed five or six petals.

Stitch through the base of the flower, through the wires, securing the petals as needed. Stitch the end of the ribbon under the flower and trim the excess. Leave the flower on the wire until the scallop has been stitched into place.

To create the scallops, starting at the top edge of the ribbon, take small tacking stitches in a wide U-shape, repeating to make five petals. See Diagram 1 below. Pull up the thread to gather. Cut off excess ribbon. Stitch to the twisted centre flower on the wire, forming a circle of petals. Remove the wire and carefully trim the base of the flower.

Diagram 1
Making the scallops

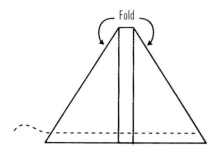

Diagram 2 Leaves
Fold the top corners down to the centre.

Diagram 3 Leaves
Gather along the lower ledge.

Buds

Insert the ribbon into the wire loop and form a rolled centre, turning five times. Pull the long end of the ribbon to the base of the roll and stitch. Cut the ribbon. Do not remove from the wire.

Work the scallop as before, making two petals, stitch around the centre roll to form a bud. Remove the wire.

Leaves

Cut the 22mm (⅞in) green ribbon into 5cm (2in) lengths. Fold the top corners down towards the centre, forming a triangle. Gather along the lower edge, pull up and fasten off. See Diagrams 2 and 3 above left.

Loop Leaves

Cut 5cm (2in) lengths of the 4mm (⅛in) green ribbon. Fold the ends towards the centre.

Fold in half to form two small loops. Stitch raw ends and centre fold together, drawing the ends of the ribbon in tightly to form 'rabbit ears'.

ASSEMBLY

Stitch or glue the flowers and leaves into place, referring to the photograph.

Using one strand of DMC gold metallic floss doubled, stitch through the lace to the right of the lowest flower on the · large motif. Tie a knot, thread through the gold heart charm, knot and tie a double bow, leaving 15mm (⅝in) tails. Stitch double bows above the large satin flower and below the top bud on the large motif. Stitch a double bow at the base of the lower flower on the small motif.

Your picture mount is now complete and ready to complement your chosen verse or photograph.

1. Pass the end of the ribbon through the wire loop, left to right.

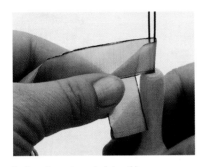

2. Turn down the end of the ribbon at a 45-degree angle.

3. Pass fold back to left side, holding ribbon in left hand.

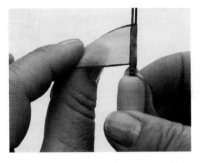

4. Turn spindle three times, winding the ribbon around both wires to form flower centre.

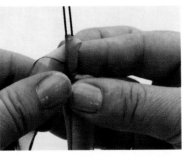

5. Holding ribbon between thumb and forefinger (thumb underneath), fold the ribbon away from the centre roll. Turn spindle with other hand, pinching base of flower to hold.

6. Continue Step 5 until you reach desired size.

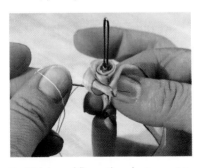

7. Stitch base of flower, through wires, up into centre of flower and back. Stitch petals as needed to secure. Stitch ribbon end under flower and remove wire. Trim excess ribbon.

8. Finished twisted rose.

Scalloped Flowers with Twisted Centres

Cherub Cushion

*This charming cushion is stitched in soft pastel shades
with silk ribbon embroidery to highlight the tiny beads,
golden cherub, diamante spider and
touches of metallic thread.*

PREPARATION

Place a piece of tracing paper over the design (page 159) and mark the centres of large roses with a dot and the large daisies with two dots. It is not necessary to transfer the entire design to your fabric, but be sure to mark the top of your tracing and the top of your fabric. A whole series of dots may not make much sense unless you know which is the right way up of the design.

Place the tracing on the fabric, and poke a hole at the dots representing the spider's web roses and daisies. Press the water-soluble pen through the holes, transferring the markings to the fabric. The rest of the flowers can be worked freehand. In this project it is not essential that every flower is in exactly the same position as on the diagram.

The cotton voile is used as a fabric stabiliser. Because it is cotton you should wash it first, as it could shrink. Then handsew the voile to the wrong side of the cushion front.

STITCHING

When using silk ribbon it is important to use lengths of 30cm (12in) or less. Do not start with a knot. Leave a tail of 1cm (⅜in) of ribbon on the wrong side of the fabric and with one thread of stranded cotton in a No 9 crewel needle, secure to the fabric with an overstitch. To finish off a ribbon, cut off about 1cm (⅜in) from the fabric and overstitch the end of the ribbon. The No 20 chenille needle is used throughout for the ribbon embroidery.

Spider's Web Roses

Work four Colonial Knots in a tight circle using dark pink ribbon. With three strands of light pink cotton, work five 4mm (⅛in) Straight Stitches evenly spaced and radiating out from the knots.

Using a 30cm (12in) length of light mushroom pink ribbon, bring the ribbon to the right side of the fabric close to the Colonial Knots at the beginning of one of the Straight Stitches. Using the eye end of your needle, weave the ribbon under and over the Straight Stitches. Do not weave the ribbon too tightly and allow it to twist naturally. Keep weaving until you have used nearly all the ribbon. Take the ribbon to the wrong side and secure.

Add the rose leaves in medium green ribbon, working loose Lazy Daisy Stitches with the holding stitch extended a little more than usual to give a good shape.

Rosebuds

With dark pink ribbon, work a Colonial Knot where indicated on the design. Embroider two Straight Stitches in light mushroom pink either side of the knot, making sure the ribbon sits flat. Take two strands of sage green thread and a No 9 crewel needle, slide the needle under the Straight Stitches of the bud and embroider a Buttonhole Stitch, taking the holding stitch back to the rose to form the

FINISHED SIZE

- 32cm x 25cm (12½in x 10in)

MATERIALS

- 35cm x 30cm (14in x 12in) mint green Zweigart Linda fabric
- 40cm x 35cm (16in x 14in) cream cotton voile
- 80cm x 115cm (⅞yd x 45in) cream cotton homespun for backing and frill
- DMC Stranded Embroidery Cotton: one skein each of sage green (523), light pink (225), medium grey (646), light fawn (842), ecru
- 4mm (⅛in) YLI silk ribbon: 3m (3¼yd) each of cream (1), blue (90), light lemon (12), grape mauve (178); 4m (4⅜yd) each of dark pink (112), light mushroom pink (157), medium green (74)
- Au Ver á Soie antique gold thread (901)
- Candlelight Colour Rainbow thread
- DMC Coton Perlé No 5 in ecru
- 25cm (10in) cream zipper
- Cream sewing thread
- Gold cherub
- 4mm (⅛in) diamanté for spider's body
- Pkt Mill Hill glass seed beads in cream (20123)
- One string small pearl beads
- No 9 and 10 crewel needle
- No 20 chenille needle
- 18cm (7in) spring hoop
- Tracing paper, pencil
- Water-soluble pen

STITCHES USED

Colonial Knot, Straight Stitch, Buttonhole Stitch,

Fly Stitch, Lazy Daisy Stitch, French Knot,

Back Stitch, Bullion Stitch,

Ribbon Stitch, Spider's Web Rose

stem of the bud. At the top of each bud, work two Straight Stitches in a V-shape, using the stranded embroidery cotton.

Cream Daisies

The petals are five large Lazy Daisy Stitches. Do not straighten the ribbon, but let it fall naturally. Using two strands of light pink stranded thread and No 9 crewel needle, work a Fly Stitch halfway up each petal, extending the holding stitch a little. Embroider three Colonial Knots in the centre of each daisy using six strands of light pink thread and No 20 chenille needle.

Add the leaves in three strands of sage green thread, working two Fly Stitches with one Straight Stitch in the centre. Do not stitch these leaves too tightly or the ribbon will lose its shape.

Rhododendrons

Using dark pink ribbon, embroider three Colonial Knots in a tight circle. Work the Lazy Daisy leaves (with extended holding stitch) around the centre knots using No 9 crewel needle and one strand of sage green thread. The number of leaves you embroider will depend on the size of the centre knots.

Ribbon Stitch Flowers

Refer to the design on page 159. Some flowers are worked in lemon and some in blue and these are marked accordingly. Work five Ribbon Stitch petals, taking care not to pull the stitch too tightly so that the tips of the petals have a soft curl and the motif will keep its shape and fullness. At the centre of each flower, sew a small pearl bead.

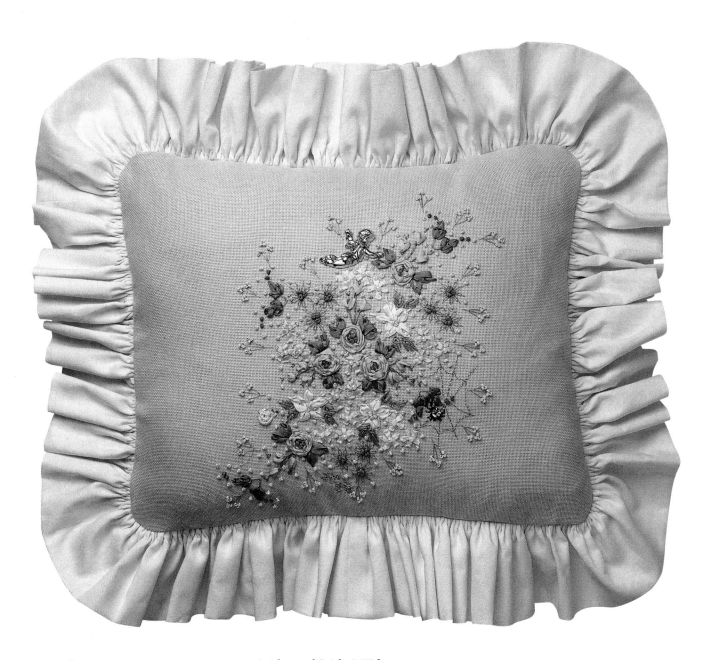

Lavender

Using grape mauve ribbon, work three 2.5mm (¹⁄₁₆in) Lazy Daisy petals with two French Knots at the tip. Finish with a Fly Stitch from one lavender to the outer in two strands of light fawn cotton.

Baby's Breath

Using one strand of sage green thread and No 10 crewel needle, embroider a Fly Stitch and extend the holding stitch a little longer than usual. Add one Straight Stitch in the centre of the Fly Stitch. Sew three seed beads on the end of each spoke. See design for placement.

Spider and Spider's Web

Using antique gold thread, Back Stitch the long cross bars, then the curved lines of the web. For the spider's body, sew the diamanté in place. Work the spider's legs either side of the diamanté in two strands of medium grey. Work a small Straight Stitch, then a smaller Straight Stitch facing towards the back of the spider to form the angle of the spider's legs.

The eyes are two Colonial Knots worked in two strands of medium grey. Finish with two Straight Stitch feelers between the eyes, also in two strands of medium grey.

Snail

For the snail shell, using ecru Perlé No 5 and No 20 chenille needle, embroider five evenly spaced 4mm (⅛in) Straight Stitches radiating from the centre. Using the eye of the needle, weave the Perlé thread under and over the Straight Stitches as you did for the Spider's Web Rose. Fill the circle with thread. The snail's body is a 15-wrap Bullion Stitch and the feelers are two Straight Stitches. Change to the gold thread and work a Colonial Knot at the end of each feeler and work some tiny Straight Stitches on the snail's shell. A finishing touch is the snail's trail worked in small Back Stitches using the Candlelight thread.

Cherub

Stitch in position using gold thread, securing with Straight Stitches around the neck, wrists, waist and ankles.

Finish with Colonial Knots scattered throughout the embroidery using ecru No 5 Perlé. Don't forget to initial and date your embroidery.

MAKING UP

Cut two pieces of cream homespun fabric, 35cm x 18cm (14in x 7in), for the cushion backing. Pin the long sides together using a 2.5cm (1in) seam allowance and leave a 25cm (10in) opening in the centre of the seam for the zipper. Sew zipper in place.

Cut three pieces of cream homespun, 15cm x 115cm (6in x 45in) and join the pieces together to form a circle, allowing 12mm (½in) seams. Fold the frill in half lengthwise, wrong sides together, and press the fold. Starting at a seam, machine-sew two rows of gathering stitch.

It is a good idea to slightly round the corners of your cushion as this makes it easier to sew on your frill. Divide the outside edge of the cushion front into quarters and mark with a pin. Divide the frill into quarters as well. Gather the frill to fit the outside edge of the cushion and match each quarter of the frill to the cushion quarters. Pin the frill around the outside of the cushion front with the fold of the frill facing towards the centre of the cushion. Adjust the gathers evenly and sew the frill to the cushion allowing a 12mm (½in) seam. Remove the pins. With the zipper opened about 10cm (4in), place the cushion back and cushion front right sides together and pin the edge.

With the cushion front facing up so you can see the stitch line of the frill, sew front and back together following the previous stitching. Open the zip fully and turn the cushion right side out.

EMBROIDERY DESIGN

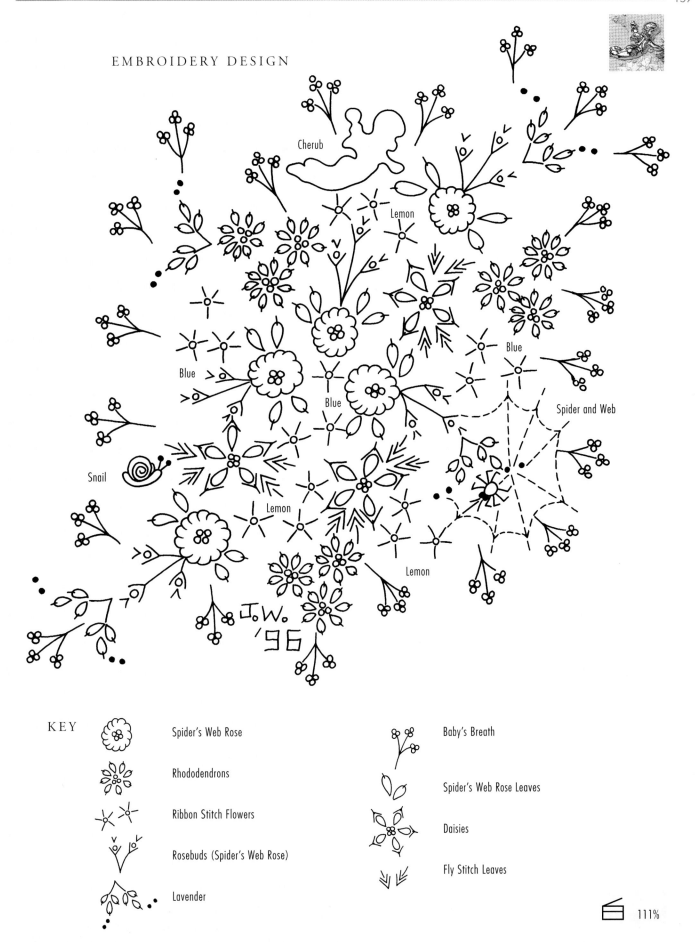

Cherub

Lemon

Blue

Blue

Blue

Spider and Web

Snail

Lemon

Lemon

J.W. '96

KEY

Spider's Web Rose

Rhododendrons

Ribbon Stitch Flowers

Rosebuds (Spider's Web Rose)

Lavender

Baby's Breath

Spider's Web Rose Leaves

Daisies

Fly Stitch Leaves

111%

Stitch Guide

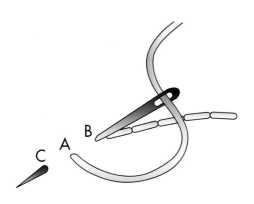

BACK STITCH

❖

Bring the needle up at A. Take a small stitch backwards and go down at B, sliding the needle to come out at C. The distance between A and B, and A and C should be equal.

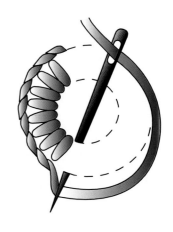

BUTTONHOLE STITCH

❖

This is worked the same way as Blanket Stitch, except the stitches are worked very close together. It is sometimes used for finishing scalloped edges or in cutwork. Also used for a decorative edging with the vertical stitches alternatively worked long and short.

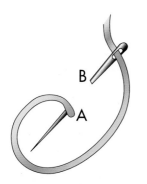 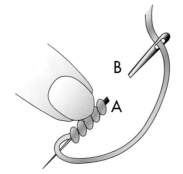 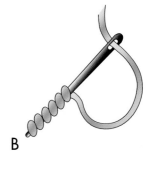

BULLION STITCH

❖

Bring the needle up at A and go down at B leaving the loop of thread on the front of the work. Bring the needle partially through the fabric at A. Wrap the needle with the loop thread (doing as many wraps as equals the distance between A and B). Gently draw the needle through the twists and use it to hold the bullion against the fabric as you pull the thread through. Take the needle to the back again at B and give a firm pull to tighten up the knot.

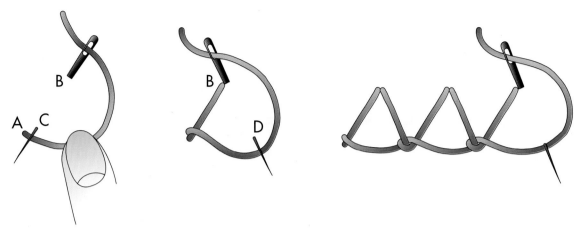

CLOSED BUTTONHOLE STITCH

This is similar to the regular Buttonhole Stitch except that the top of the side stitches are worked into the same hole (B) to form the triangle shape. Come up at A, hold the thread down with your thumb and go down at B emerging at C. Bring the needle tip over the thread and pull into place. Go down at B and form the second side stitch.

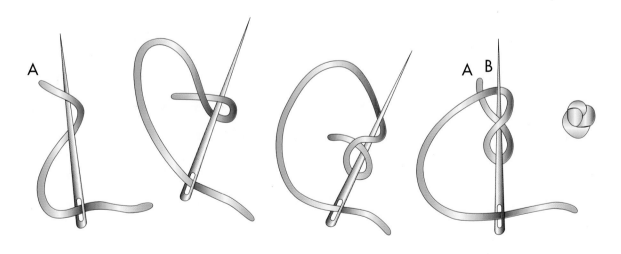

COLONIAL KNOT

Bring the needle up at A. Manipulate the needle to wrap the ribbon over, under, over and under the needle forming a figure '8'. Go back through the fabric at B (as close as possible to A). Keep the needle vertical while tightening the thread firmly around the needle. Hold the knot in place as you pull the thread through to the back.

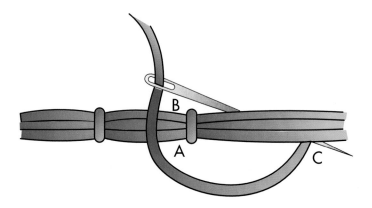

COUCHING

Couching is used to attach threads to the surface of the fabric. It is often used to attach threads too thick or textured to be stitched through the fabric. Bring out the thread to be couched at the start of the stitching line. Remove the needle and hold the thread in place with your thumb. Thread another needle with the couching thread and bring it up on the stitching line at A. Take a small stitch over the laid thread at B, bringing the needle up again at C. Repeat to the end of the stitching line, keeping your couching stitches evenly spaced. Rethread the couched thread and take it through to the back of the work and fasten off.

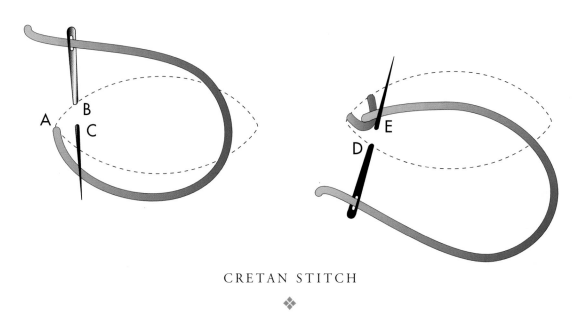

CRETAN STITCH

Work this stitch from left to right. Come up at A, go down at B and emerge at C, taking a downward vertical stitch the desired length and bringing the needle tip over the thread. Insert at D and emerge at E taking an upward vertical stitch. Be sure to keep the vertical stitches evenly spaced.

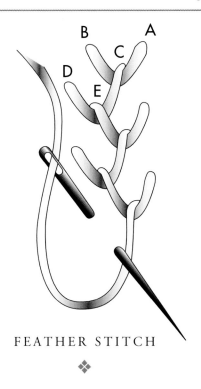

FEATHER STITCH

❖

Bring needle up at A and go down at B – even with and to the left of A – and emerge at C. Alternate the stitches back and forth, working them downwards in a vertical column. (Double Feather Stitch is worked the same way, except that two stitches are worked before the direction is changed).

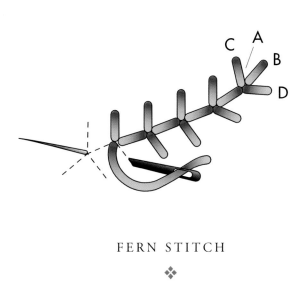

FERN STITCH

❖

Mark a line for the length of the fern leaf. Come up at A and go down at B, making a straight stitch the desired length along the line. Point A is now the pivot point for sides C and D. Come up again at A and go down at C then come up again at A and down at D, keeping the length of the stitches consistent with the first. Continue with the next stitch forming the stitch along the designated line.

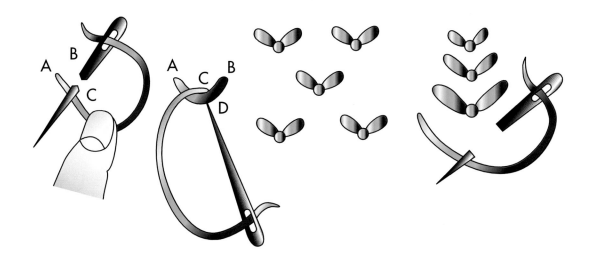

FLY STITCH

Bring the needle up at A and go down at B (to the right of and level with A), coming up again at C with the tip of the needle over the thread or ribbon. Pull the thread through the fabric and go to the back of the work again at D. This stitch can be used singly or stacked one on top of the other. The stitch from C to D can be quite small or extended.

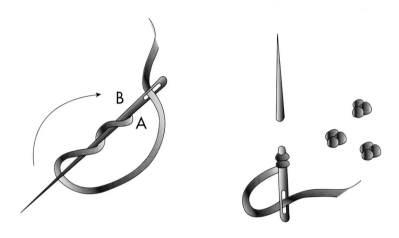

FRENCH KNOT

Bring the needle up at A and wrap the thread around the needle twice (or required number of times). Holding the thread firmly, go down at B (as close as possible to A, without actually going through the same hole). The knot should be held in place while the needle is pulled completely through to the back of the fabric.

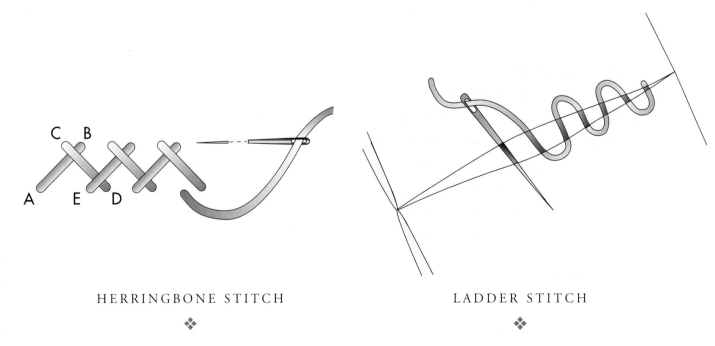

HERRINGBONE STITCH

Work from left to right. Bring the needle up at A and insert at B, sliding the needle behind the fabric to come out again at C forming a small horizontal Back Stitch. Continue working from side to side.

LADDER STITCH

Pick up a few threads of fabric along the seam line on one side, then pick up the same distance along the seam line of the other opening. The crossover thread represents the rung of the ladder, the pick-up sections the side supports.

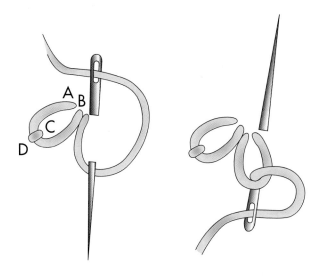

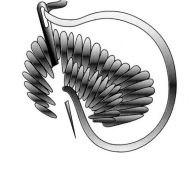

LAZY DAISY (DETACHED CHAIN)

❖

Bring the needle up at A. Slide the needle from B (as close as possible to A, but not actually through the same hole) through to C, taking the tip of the needle over the loop formed. Go down at D, creating a holding stitch.

LONG AND SHORT STITCH

❖

A dense filling stitch used when a shape is too big to be filled with regular Satin Stitch, or when shading is required. In the first row, work the stitches alternately long and short. The second and subsequent rows are all worked the same length, thus preserving the staggered appearance.

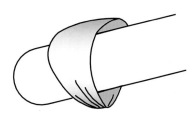

LOOP STITCH

❖

Looped straight stitch flowers are more difficult to work than most of the other flowers because the petal loops are not secured and can easily be distorted until after the centres have been worked.

Always spread the ribbon and take care not to disturb and distort the stitches as you work. You may need a second tapestry needle or cable knitting needle to slip through the ribbon loops to hold them evenly as you work.

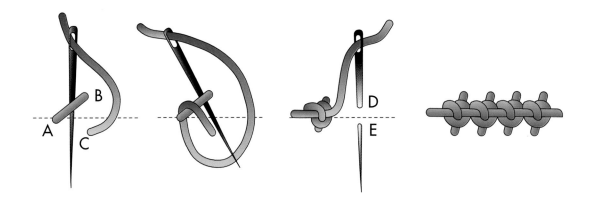

PALESTRINA STITCH

Work this stitch from left to right along the designated line. Come up at A, go down at B and emerge at C. Slide the needle under the stitch and loop the thread around the stitch bringing the needle tip over the thread. Pull the thread to form a knot, go down at D and emerge at E to continue the next stitch. Space the knots evenly and close together to give a beaded look.

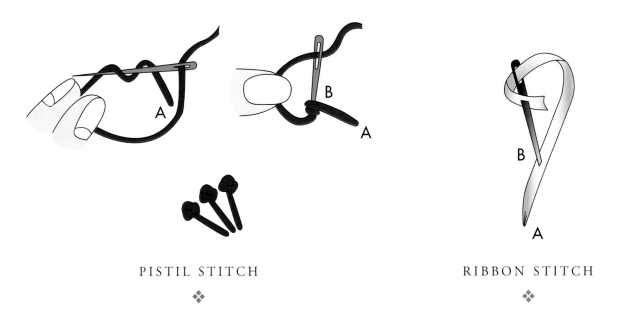

PISTIL STITCH

❖

RIBBON STITCH

❖

Bring the needle up at A, allow a short length of thread, then wrap the working thread around the needle to create a French Knot. Go down at B (this should be the length of the short thread plus the French Knot). Hold the knot in place until the needle is completely through the fabric.

Bring the needle up at A and lay the ribbon flat on the fabric. Put the needle into the middle of the ribbon at B and pull carefully through the fabric, making the edges of the ribbon curl towards the tip. Do not pull too tightly.

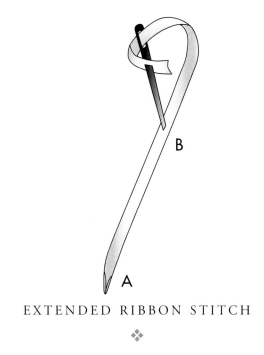

EXTENDED RIBBON STITCH

❖

This is the same as Ribbon Stitch, just slightly longer.

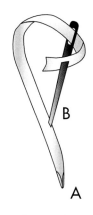

SIDE RIBBON STITCH

❖

Bring the needle up at A and lay the ribbon flat on the fabric. Put the needle into the side of the ribbon at B and pull carefully through the fabric, making the edges of the ribbon curl towards the tip. Do not pull too tightly.

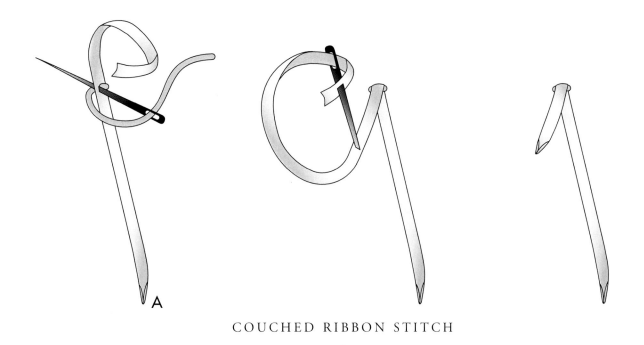

COUCHED RIBBON STITCH

❖

Come up at A. At the point where you wish the ribbon to bend, catch it with two small Straight Stitches using a cotton thread to match the ribbon. Fold the ribbon over these stitches and complete as for regular Ribbon Stitch.

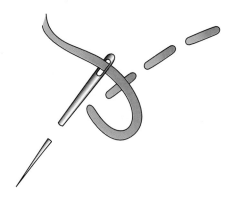

RUNNING STITCH

The thread is threaded in and out of the material along the line to be worked, keeping the stitches to an even length.

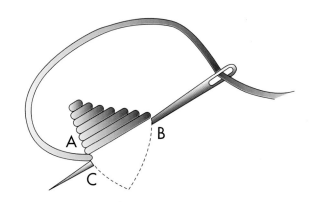

SATIN STITCH

Bring the needle up at A, go down at B and slide the needle through to C. Keep working in this manner, keeping the stitches parallel and close together until the shape has been filled.

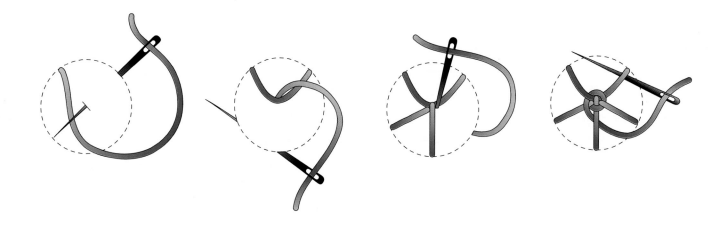

SPIDER'S WEB ROSE

Work a Fly Stitch to the desired size of the rose, having all three spokes of equal length. Add another spoke each side of the Y. You will have five spokes in all. You may choose to work French Knots in thread at the centre of the rose. If so, this should be done before the weaving. Bring your ribbon through at the centre of the spokes and work in an anti-clockwise direction, weaving the ribbon over and under the spokes. Twist the ribbon as you go, and keep it loose. Work until all the spokes are covered. If you are using more than one shade of ribbon, the deepest shade should be at the centre, graduating out to the lightest.

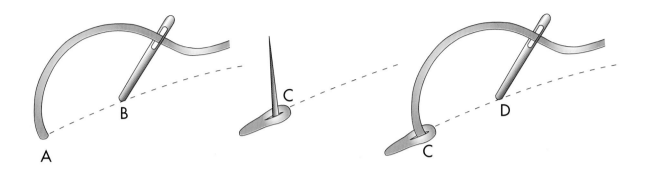

SPLIT STITCH

You will need a heavier thread for this or the thread will be difficult to split. Come up at A, make a small backward stitch to B and emerge at C piercing the working thread in half. Sometimes also called Split Back Stitch.

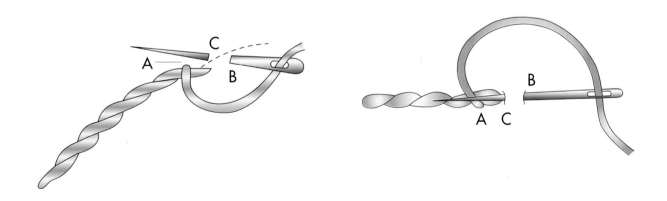

STEM STITCH: THREAD DOWN

Work from left to right. Keep the thread below the needle, come up at A and go back into the fabric at B, coming out again at C (which should be halfway along the length of the previous stitch).

STEM STITCH: THREAD UP

Work from left to right. Keep the thread above the needle, come up at A and go back into the fabric at B, coming out again at C (which should be halfway along the length of the previous stitch.

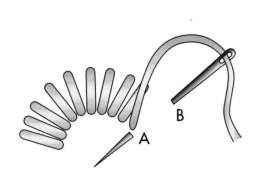

STRAIGHT STITCH

Bring the needle up at A, go down again at B. Straight stitches should be fairly firm so that they lie flat on the fabric and not too long or they may catch. They can be worked in any direction and in various lengths.

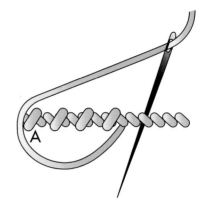

WHIPPED STEM STITCH

Refer to Stem Stitch instructions. To whip, bring the needle up at A, take the thread over the Stem Stitch and back under the next stitch, continue taking the thread over and under the foundation stitches (do not go through the fabric).

Basic Essentials

The right tools are essential for any job — and needlework is no different. There are a few essentials and some optional extras that every needleworker should have.

SCISSORS

Buy the best you can afford and look after them. Good scissors will last you a lifetime. Look for scissors that can be unscrewed and sharpened professionally.

Never, ever cut paper with scissors intended to cut fabric or thread. In fact, don't use them to cut anything but fabric or thread. Make sure the family knows your scissors are not for general use. If necessary, hide them!

Embroidery scissors should have fine blades tapering to sharp points. You will use them for cutting threads close to the fabric. Take care not to damage the points

by dropping the scissors. A scissor ball is a good idea. This is a small weight that attaches to the handles and ensures that the ball and not the points land first if the scissors are dropped.

You will also need a good pair of dressmaking scissors for cutting fabric. These should have long blades and comfortable handles.

It is also a good idea to buy or make a sheath to store the scissors when they are not in use.

HOOPS

❖

There are various kinds of hoops on the market and which one you use is largely a matter of choice. They are all designed to keep your fabric taut so there is no puckering when you stitch. It is recommended that you always remove your embroidery from the hoop when you are not actually working on it. Fabric left in a hoop for a long time may develop marks that are difficult, sometimes impossible, to remove.

The most popular style is the wooden hoop with a screw for tightening or loosening. They come in a variety of sizes from 10cm (4in) to 30cm (12in). To make sure the fabric is firmly gripped in the hoop, wrap the inner hoop with bias binding which not only helps prevent the fabric from slipping, but will also reduce the risk of marking the fabric.

Plastic spring hoops are useful for techniques that don't need the fabric to be held drum tight. They are light and convenient to use and there is no risk of snagging your fabric.

FRAMES

❖

Some embroiderers prefer rectangular frames to hoops, particularly if working on a large area.

Scroll frames come in a range of sizes, allowing a large rectangular surface to be worked on. The width of your fabric is determined by the width of the webbing or tape attached to the rollers at the top and bottom of the frame.

If working a very long project such as a bell pull, the excess fabric can be wound around the top and bottom rollers, keeping a firm tension.

Stretcher frames are made up of wooden stretcher bars which are slotted together at all the corners. Frames of different sizes can be made by combining different size bars.

Lightweight plastic frames with a semi-circular piece that snaps over a round tube are also available. These come in modular style and can be made up to various sizes, square and rectangular. As these frames can be taken apart, they are quite convenient for travelling.

FABRIC MARKERS

❖

There is a wide range of markers available. Some use permanent ink which will not wash out. Others are temporary markers – some are water soluble and others fade with exposure to light. Before marking out a design, consider which variety will best suit your purpose. Markings made by the pens that fade with light may disappear before your project is finished. A water-soluble marker may not be suitable for use on a fabric that cannot be washed. Always test your chosen marker on a scrap of fabric before marking out a whole design.

STILETTOS

❖

This is a sharp-pointed instrument used to make a hole in heavy or stiff fabric. Useful in ribbon embroidery to allow the ribbon to pass through the fabric without being crushed.

THIMBLES

Some embroiderers can't take a stitch without one, others won't wear them.

Thimbles are a matter of personal preference. They range from the economy models to sterling silver and gold-plated keepsakes. There are also ornamental thimbles which are designed to be admired rather than used.

Thimbles are particularly useful when working on heavy fabrics.

NEEDLES

❖

There are many, many needles and all are designed for a specific purpose. It is important to use the correct needle for the particular technique you are working. The size of the needle is governed by the thickness of the thread used. As a general rule, the thread should fit smoothly through the eye without distorting. Instructions usually specify the size and type of needle to use and you should follow the recommendations for the best possible result. Needle numbers refer to the size of the needle. The larger the number, the finer the needle. The most commonly used embroidery needles are crewel, chenille, straw or milliners' and tapestry needles.

Crewel needles are one of the most frequently used embroidery needles. They have a sharp point so they can easily pierce the fabric and a long slim eye to take one or more threads of stranded cotton or wool. They come in sizes 1 to 10.

Sharps are short needles with round eyes. Use for fine thread embroidery.

Straw or milliners' needles are long and the same width along the entire length of the shank. They are particularly suitable for bullion and knot stitches. They have a small, round eye which is easy to thread. Sizes range from 1 to 9.

Chenille needles have a sharp point and long eye, making them perfect for working the thicker threads and

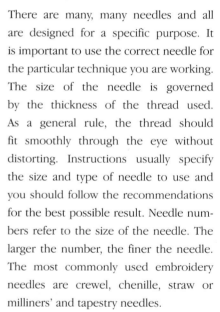

particularly suitable for candlewicking and ribbon embroidery. They come in sizes 13 to 26.

Tapestry needles have a blunt point and are most frequently used for canvaswork and cross stitch on evenweave fabrics. The blunt point passes easily through the holes in the canvas or fabric and is unlikely to pierce any thread sharing a common hole. They are also used in whipped stitches as they will slip between the fabric and stitch without snagging on the fabric. Sizes range from 18 to 26.

Beading – very fine with a minute eye that will allow the beads to slip on to the thread. They are used only for beading.

FABRICS

When choosing your background fabric, keep in mind that the ribbon has to pass through it without strain or distortion. If the weave is too tight the ribbon will be crushed. If the weave is too loose the fibres will not close around the ribbon to hold it in place.

If a fabric is too sheer the ribbon on the back of the fabric will show through. Should your fabric need backing, use a very light fabric such as silk organza, fine silks or cottons.

The choice of natural fabric, blended or synthetic is determined by the use of the finished article. Since silk ribbon embroidery cannot be ironed without crushing it, fabrics that require little or no ironing after washing are the most practical to use. If you do wash your finished article, test all fabric and ribbons for colour fastness. Silk ribbon embroidery can be drycleaned, but remember to request the cleaner not to press it.

Linen, cotton, homespun or calico, silk, satin, damask and even lightweight fabrics like voile are suitable for hand embroidery. Basically, the fabric must have enough body to support the weight of the embroidery and the weave should be firm enough to hold the thread.

A sheer fabric like voile requires a fine thread. Care must be taken that threads on the back do not show through to the front, causing a shadow effect.

Another point to consider when choosing fabric is whether your fabric has a matt or shiny finish and whether there is sufficient contrast between the fabric and the threads to be used.

Linen, calico and damask can be laundered. Silk and satin should be drycleaned. Any fabric that has a tendency to fray – linen and silk, particularly – should be overlocked or hand overcast before you commence your embroidery. An alternative is to use an anti-fray product.

Velvet and velveteen both offer a rich background, particularly for silk ribbon embroidery. Dress-weight fabrics have a base cloth that is not too closely woven and allows the ribbon to pass through easily. When working with threads on plush fabrics, care must be taken that the thread is thick and colourful enough enough to sit on the surface of the pile and not disappear into it.

Wool, cotton and linen are all suitable for embroidery with either silk ribbon or thread. Look for fabrics that are woven firmly enough to hold the threads. If using a loosely woven fabric you may need to add a backing fabric to stabilise it and to prevent the stitches on the reverse side showing through to the front of the work.

Silk is a luxurious background for special projects; moire, dupion, Thai silk, taffeta, shot taffeta and satin are all suitable weights for framed pictures, cushions, clothing and many kinds of fashion accessories.

From T-shirt fabric to winter-weight jerseys, knits are all suitable for ribbon embroidery, but will need a stabiliser on the back to prevent puckering.

Synthetics and blends, because they need little or no ironing, can work well for ribbon embroidery on items that will need to be washed.

LAUNDERING

If the fabric requires washing, prewash it before starting work to allow for possible shrinkage. To wash, gently hand wash using pure soap, rinse well, then dry it in the shade. When ironing, take care to avoid the embroidery. If the ribbon appears flat, lightly spray it with water and it will sit up as if it has just been completed.

THREADS

Stranded cottons, sometimes called floss, are probably the most popular of all embroidery threads. They come in an extensive range of colours and, although most are colour fast, it is a good idea to test for fastness if you are making an item that will require washing. Stranded cottons are composed of six threads and can be used whole or separated into the number of strands required. If separating, cut the required length, then separate one thread at a time. Hold up the thread and allow it to untwist before putting together the number of threads you require. This helps the thread to sit well on the fabric and prevents twisting and tangling. You can also blend two or more colours to create subtle threads. Stranded cottons come in a range of plain colours and variegated shades.

There are also stranded threads in pure silk and synthetics. These have a rich lustre and can be used whole, or separated and blended as when using stranded cottons.

Rayon threads are used for Brazilian embroidery and have a lustrous finish. They need to be handled differently from other threads and instructions for Brazilian embroidery projects usually include this information.

Wools come in tapestry and crewel weights. If a finer wool is needed use crewel wool rather than trying to split tapestry wool. Both come in a huge range of colours.

Perlé or pearl thread is a pure cotton two-ply that is twisted to produce a beaded effect.

Available in weights from a thick No 3 through the middleweights, No 5 and 8, to a fine No 12. These have a good lustre and come in a wide colour range but not all colours are available in all weights.

Hand-dyed threads are available in wool, silk and cotton, in both plain colours and overdyes. If the project is likely to require more than one skein of these threads, make sure you purchase the same dyelot. Being hand-dyed, the colours may vary considerably between the various dyelots.

RIBBONS

❖

Pure silk ribbon is soft and pliable, with a surface that looks the same on both sides. Available in widths from 2mm (¹⁄₁₆in) up to 32mm (1½in) with the most used widths being 2mm (¹⁄₁₆in), 4mm (⅛in) and 7mm (¼in). If you are buying ribbon without an actual project in mind – just because you've seen it and been attracted to the colour, for instance – 2m (2¼yd) is a practical amount to buy in most colours. Green ribbon, which you will tend to use a lot for foliage could be purchased in larger amounts.

Sheer ribbons, such as the synthetic organdies, can be used alone or in combination with another ribbon. They can be used to create shadow effects that lend perspective to your work and are suitable for folding as well as embroidery.

Synthetic ribbons made of 100 per cent Azlon look like silk ribbons, but have more spring than silk and will not lie as flat against the fabric. Available in 3.5mm (⅛in) and 7mm (¼in) widths in a wide range of plain colours. There is also a range of Azlon ombre ribbon in the 3.5mm (⅛in) width and a picot-edged 6mm (¼in) polyester ombre ribbon. Plain polyester ribbons come in many colours and widths.

Double-sided polyester satin ribbon comes in widths from 1.5mm (¹⁄₁₆in) to 90mm (3½in). Heavier and shinier than silk ribbon, it is suitable for making folded roses, concertina roses, free-form flowers and leaves. The narrowest satin ribbon can be couched to form branches and stems. The use of a stiletto is recommended if you wish to use polyester satin ribbon for embroidery.

Cotton organdy is made from 100 per cent pure cotton and is available only in 9mm (⅜in) width. This ribbon has an open mesh finish. An interesting texture that could be used to weave baskets for flower pictures.

MORE ESSENTIALS

You will find round plastic or wooden toothpicks or fine knitting needles are useful to control the size of loop stitches.

Index

Embroidery projects are in italics